D0918553

METHODS
OF
MADNESS

The Mental Hospital as a Last Resort

Benjamin M. Braginsky
Cushing Hospital

Dorothea D. Braginsky
Fairfield University

Kenneth Ring
University of Connecticut

UNIVERSITY
PRESS OF
AMERICA

Library of Congress Catalog Card Number: 81-40099

To our parents

Preface

Upon visiting a mental institution, it would not be surprising to observe that many patients are "out of touch with reality," failing to perceive discrepancies between their beliefs and external events. But it would be amazing, indeed, to discover that a large number of the professionals concerned with the "mentally ill" (psychiatrists and psychologists, for example) manifest such a perceptual deficit. *We have been amazed.*

As social psychologists we translated this reaction into a systematic investigation and critique of current psychiatric dogma. The purpose of this book is twofold. First, we attempted to portray, as faithfully as possible, the mental patient as he is and how he lives. Second, we examined critically from both theoretical and empirical bases the prevalent psychiatric conception of mental illness.

Surely we are not the first to challenge the validity of psychiatric theories and practices; this has been done by using theoretical, historical, and linguistic perspectives. Our book, however, offers empirical substance to the attack through nine interrelated studies ranging from controlled experimentation to ecological investigations. The objective here was not only to demonstrate the untenability of current psychiatric modes of thought but also to present a meaningful alternative to the understanding and the "treatment" of the people who are called mentally ill.

The research presented in this book was conducted at a large state mental hospital in New England, where the senior author and prime mover of all this research, Benjamin Braginsky, was a research social psychologist. The book was written, however, while he was a research staff psychologist at Yale University (under HEW grant HDO 3008-01), while Dorothea Braginsky was a research associate at the Veterans Administration Hospital in West Haven, Connecticut, and while Kenneth Ring was an associate professor at the University of Connecticut.

We would like to express our appreciation to our friends and colleagues who both read the manuscript and gave thoughtful suggestions concerning it: Drs. Rudolph Abramczyk, Herbert Cross, Alan Fontana, Karl Hakmiller, Harold Kelley, Jacob Levine, Daniel Levinson, Donald Mosher, John Rakusin, Elizabeth Ring, Alan Towbin, and Edward Zigler. For their assistance in facilitating our research we thank Hector Arbor, Lawrence Finison, Martin Grosse, Denis Ridley, and Doris Seiler. For typing the original manuscript we thank Linda Swartz. We would like to acknowledge Theodore Sarbin for his help in the preparation of the manuscript and particularly for his suggestion of our main title. We especially want to acknowledge Dr. John Turner for his invaluable help throughout the research program. Without the encouragement, intellectual stimulation, and conducive environment that Jules Holzberg provided this research could not have been accomplished.

And for the nurture and patience that Marilyn Braginsky gave to us during this period, which helped make this book possible, an especially warm thank-you.

B.M.B.

D.D.B.

K.R.

Middletown, Conn.
January 1969

Contents

Introduction

As a clinical psychologist for more than twenty-five years, it has been an exciting experience to be on the periphery of the development and implementation of the ideas and research reported in this volume. As one who has been reared in the psychiatric orientation to deviant behavior, my own reactions can be sequentially described as apprehension, euphoria, and finally realistic appreciation. I stress the sequence of these reactions because they may be similar to those of some, if not many, of the readers of this volume.

My initial reaction of apprehension was rooted in the recognition that the ideas being proposed were a challenge to a "way of professional life" in which I had been trained and to which I was committed even though I recognized the limitations of the psychiatric model after a quarter of a century of involvement in a variety of psychiatric settings. A challenge to a "way of life" inevitably arouses uneasiness, and I must confess that such were my feelings when this program of research and its rationale were first broached. I remember offering what I considered to be appropriate theoretical considerations in opposition to some of the ideas being advanced, but it soon came to dawn upon me that some of my "resistances" were less than rational. I found myself defending the psychiatric model in spite of my oft-repeated observations of its limitations. It seemed as if I needed to resist because I sensed a potential threat in these new ideas. That "threat," I now believe, was to that way of professional life and its assumptions which had become too well integrated into my sense of self. Similar resistances by professionals have been described by Miller (1964) and Riessman and Miller (1964).

Once I was able to reduce my uneasiness and could rationally accept the need for alternate models in the context of the limitations of the psychiatric model, I found myself caught up in a state of euphoric excitement, in part buttressed by empirical research that supported the authors' contentions. During this phase, my thinking underwent dramatic change, and I now felt that I was observing the evolvement of a model of deviant behavior that could and would become the "new religion" for those having responsibility for deviant people. In part, I responded to the helplessness that grows out of the experience with the psychiatric model with its many failures of treatment, particularly in the hospital setting. Here was a new formulation that would lead to new understanding of deviancy and new ways of coping with it.

Finally, I settled into a phase of more sober reflection that permitted me to more realistically assess the body of conceptualization and research reported here. Such reflection has compelled me to recognize this report as a significant, scholarly work that is opening a new door to the understanding of those who have traditionally been labeled "mentally ill." I use the singular term "door" because I am sure the authors would agree that the ultimate understanding of "the mentally ill" will require the opening of many doors. The research data presented here are impressive but, in the language of research, they leave much variance still unexplained. What is significant and unique about this report is that it gives saliency to several aspects of behavior that have been systematically ignored in our current conceptualizations of the mental patient, and it provides a body of challenging, supportive research data. In the best tradition of the science of psychology, it offers a new conceptualization which has been tested with re-markable success in the cauldron of research. Building upon this work, the authors and others can help to define those doors that need opening as we approach the ultimate goal of a comprehensive theory of the hospitalized mental patient.

The practices that have developed for coping with the deviant person, however they may have varied throughout history, have been rooted in prevailing assumptions regarding deviancy. These assumptions have varied in terms of their explicitness and their rationality. We need not detail this history, for this is available to the interested reader in many sources (for example, Alexander and Selesnick, 1966; Zilboorg and Henry, 1941; Deutsch, 1946). What needs to be stressed is the intimate relationship between the philosophy of man prevailing in a given historical period and the assumptions concerning the deviant person. What is of importance is the relationship between these assumptions and the institutionalized practices that have developed for coping with deviance.

A basic assumption operative in at least the present century has been that the deviant person is cognitively impaired (ego-defective) and thus ineffectual and incapable of exercising options. This assumption has led inevitably to an institutional device (the mental hospital) to provide compensations for ego deficiencies. Once the patient is hospitalized, this assumption has further dictated a set of practices within the hospital that have become the subject of much recent criticism because of their authoritarianism (Holzberg, 1960), degradation (Sarbin, 1967), dehumanization (Goffman, 1961) and illness-maintenance (Schwartz, 1960).

The report presented here challenges the assumption of patient ineffectuality. Rather it documents the extraordinary capacity of hospitalized patients to exercise options and thus influence their fates. To some this may not be a startling discovery, for clinical experiences have provided opportunities to observe hospitalized patients inhibiting symptom expression in order to be discharged, while other patients exaggerate symptoms in order to influence staff decisions with regard to remaining in the hospital. Without defending Freudian theory in its entirety, it is of interest to observe that Freud (1936) recognized that symptoms, while emerging in the service of anxiety reduction (primary gain), often assumed gratifying values because of their influence on the social world (secondary gain). What is significant about the current report's conception of the mental patient is that admission to and retention in the mental hospital are seen to be more a function of the "secondary" purpose of symptoms rather than their "primary" purpose. For the authors, symptoms are behavior to control outcomes in a social situation—they are a form of social communication. As such, they represent no special category of behavior that needs to be distinguished from other behaviors serving the same function of controlling outcomes. Moreover, the report offers evidence that this utilization of symptoms need not be outside of awareness, but may reflect the deliberate efforts of the patient to attain his established goal with regard to institutionalization.

This leads the authors to conclude that assumptions regarding the mental patient need be no different than those explaining the nonhospitalized person—both can be seen as motivated to attain their established goals. The authors do not suggest that there are no individual differences in the success with which people attain goals, but they are insistent that such varying degrees of success characterize people who are labeled as mentally ill as well as those not so labeled.

While Freud, as an example of a clinical theorist, developed his systematic position to explicate both normal and deviant behavior, there is little question but that current clinical practice sorts people (normal, neurotic, psychotic, and so on) and that differing assumptions embodying value judgments ensue from this labeling process. I do not believe that the authors are objecting to the process of classification as a necessary step in the development of a science of behavior. Rather they are objecting to a system of classification that leads to value judgments regarding persons in each classification.

It may be argued that the ideas presented here are not yet ready to account for the total population of deviant people. The subjects of the research have been principally hospitalized patients, which surely supports the assumptions put forth by the authors regarding in-patients. It seems hazardous, however, to generalize from this population to that large bulk of deviant persons, that is, neurotics, character problems, ambulatory psychotics, and so on, who never seek or receive hospitalization during their lives. This is not to suggest that such theorizing as advanced here may not in the future be empirically demonstrated to be applicable to such groups. Clearly, some neurotics, character disorders, and so on, do become in-patients and it may be, as the authors suggest, that hospitalization and nonhospitalization occur less for reasons of severity of behavior deviation than for the patient motives delineated by the authors. While it may be that much of what the authors detail may eventually be applicable to these groups, limiting the generalization now to hospitalized patients is nevertheless a significant contribution. The Joint Commission on Mental Illness and Health (1961) has stated that this is the major mental health problem, and it would seem that the present research goes far to illuminate the hospital patient in ways that have only been minimally suggested up to now.

It would be unfortunate if the reader were to sense from this report an attitude of callousness toward hospital patients or nihilism with regard to the problem of mental illness. Such an interpretation is possible because the authors describe the hedonic nature of certain patient adaptation styles which are designed to illuminate the tenaciousness with which patients pursue their goals regarding hospitalization. It should be stressed, however, that the authors are not suggesting that hospitalized patients are in this sense different from any other persons, including nonpatients. All people committed to goals may pursue them with vigor and determination. This leads the authors to their central theme—patients and nonpatients are alike in their pursuit of goals, and this emphasis leaves one with a deeper respect for the mental patient. If I may be so bold as to reflect what I view as the authors' values, they are stressing in their thinking and in their research the essential humanness of the patient and his identity with all men. Their quarrel is not with the mental patient, but with those assumptions that have led to the patient's being viewed differently and less humanly than nonpatients. Theirs is a compassionate concern for the patient that would lead to more constructive modes of dealing with the person who seeks refuge from the larger society. Perhaps their focus on how patients are similar to nonpatients, in sharp contrast to the more contemporary focus on how patients differ from nonpatients, is part of the emerging cultural and intellectual climate that has awakened us to how we have dealt differently with blacks and poor humans, and has demanded that these groups be viewed in a context that does not accentuate their differences from nonblacks and the nonpoor.

Psychology has a special burden to bear within this particular context. Its focus on group differences has tended to sharpen the study of differences and to ignore the similarities between men. One must caution, of course, against a search for similarities that can degenerate into support for conformity. In the context of this argument, I do not fear this consequence in the case being presented by the authors. They are speaking to a need to recognize important motives of the mental patient as being analogous to those in the nonpatient. In so doing, and in demonstrating that these motives rather than "illness" variables such as diagnosis and social history are predictors of such criteria as discharge, length of hospitalization, and so on, they are challenging the accepted view that "illness" alone can explain the processes of institutionalization and discharge.

There is ample documentation to the effect that traditional mental health programs have not fared well with large segments of our people, particularly the poor (Hollingshead and Redlich, 1958; Riessman, Cohen and Pearl, 1964). Many explanations have been advanced for this phenomenon, including differences between the professional and the poor person in terms of general values, mental health ideology, and so on. However, it may be that our mental health services, rooted in the clinical tradition of delineating differences that lead to labeling (diagnosing), are somehow incompatible with the poor person's search to be like others who are not poor. This is at best a speculation, but deserves further thinking if there is validity to the thesis that a different philosophy underlies a psychology of differences than a psychology of similarities.

The present report raises a serious question regarding research conducted with hospitalized patients. The evidence presented here demonstrates that patient responses on psychological tests and in interviews are significantly affected by the motives of the patient as they pertain to hospitalization, interacting with the patient's perceptions of the purposes of the tests and interviews. That psychologists are aware of many factors, other than the stimulus variables of test and interview items, influencing a subject's performance is well established. Included are situational and interpersonal variables (Masling, 1960), expectations and biases of the examiner (Orne, 1962; Rosenthal, 1966), and so on. But the emphasis in this report on responses of the patient being influenced by his desire to effect a certain outcome with regard to hospitalization must of necessity raise many doubts about findings based on hospitalized patients. Thus, the substantial body of findings depicting chronic schizophrenics as impaired in a variety of functions (for example, Shakow, 1962) can perhaps shed more light on patients' motives than on the condition of chronic schizophrenia itself. Further research with this variable in mind should help to clarify the extent to which it has been involved in influencing our present body of research data and theorizing (Fontana and Klein, 1968).

In developing a taxonomy of patient styles of adaptation to the hospital, the authors have added their voices to those of others who have questioned the adequacy and the appropriateness of the mental hospital, and its more recent derivative—the Mental Health Center—as the institutional framework to provide for the needs of all deviant people (Albee, 1963; Glasscote and others, 1964; Smith and Hobbs, 1966). These different styles of adaptation speak to differing needs of deviant people, and these needs may more appropriately be met by a range of institutional structures designed for these specific needs. In delineating a pitifully small number of patients motivated by what the professional calls "therapeutic" goals, they speak eloquently to the need for other social structures to adequately deal with these people's conditions, although they make explicit only one such social institution—the cooperative retreat. While we are now seeing some attempts in this direction in terms of halfway houses (Raush and Raush, 1968), the cooperative retreat is an exciting possibility that should be fully implemented.

What emerges with clarity is that a large proportion of patients seek the hospital as a refuge from the world in which they are reluctant to be social participants. Such a finding propels intensive examination of those social conditions that give rise to such an orientation. The work of the authors may well fuse with that of those studying the poor and the underprivileged (Clausen, 1966; Fried, 1964), and we may yet discover that for many people whom we have labeled schizophrenic, we are merely "psychologizing" the social phenomena of poverty, discrimination, and powerlessness, of which we are now appropriately hearing more (Hollingshead and Redlich, 1958; Pasamanick and others, 1964; McDermott and others, 1965). There is more than the suggestion that for many such people hospitalization may be the only alternative to such debilitating social conditions and the only available escape from their dehumanization.

While there has been much written about the dehumanization and antitherapeutic attitudes inherent in the practices of total institutions including mental hospitals (Goffman, 1961), the theorizing of the authors suggests that hospitalization for certain people is far less a dehumanizing process than is that of the social conditions from which mental patients are drawn. This argument is not intended by the authors, I am sure, to insist that variations in social conditions account for all the variance in human behavior. While it is not entirely explicit from their report, personality variables also account for some of the variance among people. The emphasis, as I read it, is that clinical practice has so overwhelmingly stressed personality factors to the exclusion of social conditions that some sharp antidote is necessary. What research we have available indicates that it is the interaction of personality factors and social conditions that accounts maximally for behavioral variance (Hunt, 1965).

For the authors, the construct of "mental illness" is not only a "myth" (Szasz, 1961) but, because of its intrinsic assumptions, is a vehicle for devaluing the humanness of those so labeled. The descriptions accruing to the labeled person are essentially negative. I have not heard anyone describe such persons in positive terms except for Rank (Karpf, 1953) who speaks of the deviant, within his will theory, as one who is striving to become the creative artist (the highest level of adaptation) but who has not yet succeeded. In this regard, the deviant is a superior person to "the average man." It is such devaluation that ensues from the label "mentally ill" today, together with this insistence by the authors on the identity of goals, that compels the authors to reject the construct "mentally ill."

Thus, I see the present work as a portent for the development of new institutional structures and new practices growing out of an ideology that views the psychiatric model and its derivatives of the hospital and "treatment" methods as no longer conceptually appropriate to the needs of people who have been hospitalized (Caplan, 1964; Sarason and others, 1966). Hopefully, such new thinking will lead to more effective "prevention" than has yet been possible. What is being presented here is a challenge to the long-held view that the so-called mental health problem can best be met by more hospitals (or more recently, mental health centers) and more professional staff to render therapeutic services, a challenge being expressed by other writers (Kelley, 1966; Nichols, 1963; Duhl, 1965). The startling data on the small number of "therapeautically oriented" patients challenge this as the need. Surely there is a need for refuge for distraught, frustrated, and discriminated people, but the hospital and its emphasis on "treatment" does not seem the answer to this significant need. As Cowen (1967) indicates, our treatment approaches are centered on the "giving of help." But yet, most mental patients are like the poor, seeking not help but the opportunity to escape and be released from the debilitating social conditions in which they are locked.

The assumptions of the psychiatric model have led to a social system for dealing with the deviant person (the mental hospital), to a principal emphasis on giving help to affect behavior change (psychotherapy), and to a delineation of roles dictated by these. The model advanced in this report not only questions the primacy of the mental hospital and of psychotherapy, but surely has implications for the kinds of roles needed for coping with the problem of social deviance. While these changed or new roles are not immediately apparent, it is surely an inevitable consequence of a model that so drastically deviates from the psychiatric one. If such a model permits the identification of those social pressures that compel a person to seek refuge, this may help to indicate the types of roles necessary to cope with the problem. Recent evidence pointing to the effects of poverty, discrimination, housing, and education on personality have pointed to new roles that can be filled by classes of people hitherto not considered for such roles (Duhl, 1965; Schofield, 1964; Kelley, 1964). Perhaps more importantly, such knowledge may influence even the roles of professionals, for as Cowen (1967) suggests, we may see the emergence of "preventing professions" as distinct from "helping professions."

I must once again state that the report that follows is an important contribution to the ideological controversy in which the mental health field finds itself today. The need for "open minds" at this critical juncture cannot be overemphasized if we are to extricate ourselves from the danger of committing the same errors in the next fifty years that we have in the last fifty years. This does not deny the liberating role played by the psychiatric model in instituting more humane care for the mentally ill following the era of demonoligical conceptions of deviant behavior. However, we must beware of its becoming a barrier to further progress (Eisenberg, 1962).

Many of our assumptions (and even theories) about deviance may yet fall by the wayside under the scrutiny of research evidence. [A research program in which I have been involved has raised serious questions about our assumptions regarding the families of schizophrenics (Farina and Holzberg, 1967, 1968).] This volume reports a new approach to viewing the mental patient, tests this view with sound research data, and charts possible new directions for movement. Never was there a greater need for systematic expounding of alternate views to the psychiatric model. The present volume is an important contribution that is likely to influence the field in the foreseeable future.

JULES D. HOLZBERG

REFERENCES

Albee, G. W., American psychology in the sixties. *American Psychologist, 18:* 90–95, 1963.

Alexander, F. G., and S. T. Selesnick, *The History of Psychiatry.* New York: Harper & Row, Publishers, 1966.

Caplan, G., The role of pediatricians in community mental health (with particular reference to the primary prevention of mental disorders in children). In L. Bellak (ed.), *Handbook of Community Psychiatry and Community Mental Health.* New York: Grune & Stratton, Inc., 1964, pp. 287–299.

Clausen, J. A., A sociological perspective. In R. Brockbank and D. Westby-Gibson (eds.), *Mental Health in a Changing Community.* New York: Grune & Stratton, Inc., 1966. Pp. 13–17.

Cowen, E. I., Emergent approaches to mental health problems: an overview and directions for future work. In E. L. Cowen, E. A. Gardner and M. Zax (eds.), *Emergent Approaches to Mental Health Problems.* New York: Appleton-Century-Crofts, 1967.

Deutsch, A., *The Mentally Ill in America.* New York: Columbia University Press, 1946.

Duhl, L. J., The psychiatric evolution. In S. E. Goldston (ed.), *Concepts of Community Psychiatry: A Framework for Training.*

Bethesda, Md.: U.S. Dept. of H.E.W., Public Health Serv. Public. No. 1319, 1965, pp 19–32.

Eisenberg, L., Possibilities for a preventive psychiatry. *Pediatrics, 30:* 815–828, 1962.

Farina, A. and J. D. Holzberg, Attitudes and behaviors of fathers and mothers of male schizophrenic patients. *Journal of Abnormal Psychology, 72:* 381–387, 1967.

Farina, A. and J. D. Holzberg, Interaction patterns of parents and hospitalized sons diagnosed as schizophrenic or nonschizophrenic. *Journal of Abnormal Psychology, 73:* 114–118, 1968.

Fontana, A. F. and E. B. Klein, Self-presentation and the schizophrenic "deficit." *Journal of Consulting and Clinical Psychology, 32:* 250–256, 1968.

Freud, S., *The Problem of Anxiety.* New York: W. W. Norton & Company, Inc., 1936.

Fried, M., Social problems and psychopathology. In *Urban America and the Planning of Mental Health Services.* New York: Group for Advancement of Psychiatry, 1964, pp. 404–446.

Glasscote, R. M., D. Sanders, H. M. Forstenzer, and A. R. Foley, *The Community Mental Health Center: An Analysis of Existing Models.* Washington, D.C.: Amer. Psychiat. Assn., 1964.

Goffman, E., *Asylums.* New York: Doubleday & Company, Inc., 1961.

Hollingshead, A. B. and F. C. Redlich, *Social Class and Mental Illness: A Community Study.* New York: John Wiley & Sons, Inc., 1958.

Holzberg, J. D., The historical traditions of the state hospital as a force of resistance to the team. *American Journal of Orthopsychiatry, 30:* 87–94, 1960.

Hunt, J. McV., Traditional personality theory in the light of recent evidence. *American Scientist, 53:* 80–96, 1965.

Joint Commission on Mental Illness and Health, *Action for Mental Health.* New York: Basic Books, Inc., 1961.

Karpf, F. B., *The Psychology and Psychotherapy of Otto Rank.* New York: Philosophical Library, Inc., 1953.

Kelley, J. G., The mental health agent in the urban community. In *Urban America and the Planning of Mental Health Services.* New York: Group for Advancement of Psychiatry, 1964. Pp. 474–494.

Kelley, J. G., Ecological constraints on mental health services. *American Psychologist, 21:* 535–539, 1966.

Masling, J. M., The influence of situational and interpersonal variables in projective testing. *Psychological Bulletin, 57:* 65–85, 1960.

McDermott, J. F., S. I. Harrison, J. Schrager and P. Wilson, Social class and mental illness: observations of blue collar families.

American Journal of Orthopsychiatry, 35: 500–508, 1965.

Miller, S. M., Social class, mental illness, and American psychiatry: An expository review. In F. Reissman, J. Cohen, and A. Pearl (eds.), *Mental Health of the Poor*. New York: Free Press, 1964. Pp. 11–15.

Nichols, R. S., The influence of economic and administrative factors on the type and quality of care given to persons with psychological disease. *Working Papers in Community Mental Health, 1:* 1–34, 1963.

Orne, M. T., On the social psychology of the psychological experiment: with particular reference to demand characteristics and their implications. *American Psychologist, 17:* 776–783, 1962.

Pasamanick, B., D. W. Roberts, P. W. Lemkau, and D. B. Krueger, A survey of mental disease in an urban population: prevalence by race and income. In F. Riessman, J. Cohen, and A. Pearl (eds.), *Mental Health of the Poor*. New York: Free Press, 1964. Pp. 38–48.

Raush, H. L., and C. L. Raush, *The Halfway House Movement: A Search for Sanity*. New York: Appleton-Century-Crofts, 1968.

Riessman, F., J. Cohen, and A. Pearl (eds.), *Mental Health of the Poor*. New York: Free Press, 1964.

Riessman, F., and S. M. Miller, Social change versus the "psychiatric world view." *American Journal of Orthopsychiatry, 34:* 29–38, 1964.

Rosenthal, R., *Experimenter Effects in Behavioral Research*. New York: Appleton-Century-Crofts, 1966.

Sarason, S. B., M. Levine, I. I. Goldenberg, D. L. Cherlin, and E. M. Bennett, *Psychology in Community Settings*. New York: John Wiley & Sons., Inc., 1966.

Sarbin, T. R., On the futility of the proposition that some people be labeled "mentally ill." *Journal of Consulting Psychology, 31:* 447–453, 1967.

Schofield, W., *Psychotherapy: The Purchase of Friendship*. Englewood Cliffs, N.J.: Prentice-Hall, Inc., 1964.

Schwartz, M. S., Functions of the team in the state mental hospital. *American Journal of Orthopsychiatry, 30:* 100–102, 1960.

Shakow, D., Segmental set: A theory of the psychological deficit in schizophrenia. *Archives of General Psychiatry, 6:* 1–17, 1962.

Smith, M. B., and N. Hobbs, The community and the community mental health center. *American Psychologist, 21:* 499–509, 1966.

Szasz, T. S., *The Myth of Mental Illness*. New York: Hoeber-Harper, 1961.

Zilboorg, G., and G. W. Henry, *A History of Medical Psychiatry*. New York: W. W. Norton & Company, Inc., 1941.

A Day in the Life
of a Schizophrenic

NAME: *Carol Cardin*   AGE: *37*   SEX: *Female*
LENGTH OF PRESENT HOSPITALIZATION: *19 months*
DIAGNOSIS: *Schizophrenic*

Q. Name as many places in the hospital as you can that you can
spend time in.

A. Well, the canteen in Bolin, the canteen in Farmer Hall, the
chapel, the multipurpose room here in Bolin Hall . . . course,
on our ward spend most of the time, and in the chapel I spend
a good deal of time typing and taking shorthand for Mr.
Rogers. Well, there is the Moore Shop that they visit—I've

never visited there. The garden—they have a garden over there that they let patients come in and look around once in a while. It's in a greenhouse. I think I've gone there once. Of course, you can walk around the grounds—we take many walks.

Q. What do most of the patients do in these places? For example, the canteen, the coffee shop.

A. Waste time! That's the biggest thing on our hands. It's just a matter of wasting time. Of course, a lot of places like the small canteen and the large canteen, you can bring people who have come to see you, and it's a nicer place than just sitting on the ward.

Q. When you say waste time, what do they really do?

A. Oh, they have something to eat, a cup of coffee.

Q. How about these other places, like the chapel? What do most patients do there?

A. Oh, they would visit the chapel, pray, go to mass if they're Catholic, and just make visits.

Q. What do most patients do in the Moore Shop?

A. There are articles given to the hospital; ex-patients and people from charities and all and individuals bring clothes up here that are no longer useful or that don't fit them anymore. And they're given to the Moore Shop. And the Moore Shop allows the patients to go in and pick and choose what they would like to have or what might fit them, as far as clothes and pocketbooks and shoes and hats and things like that.

Q. What do most patients do on the ward?

A. Watch television or just sit there. Some of them just sit there, and you wonder how they can sit there for five, six, seven hours, just looking into space and not doing anything. They're just living vegetables! That's why I couldn't stand it and I had to have a job. And Mrs. Sarah got me a job with Mr. Rogers, and from then on I've been happy—relatively happy, if you can be happy away from your home and all.

Q. Where do most patients go when they walk around? Where do they spend time?

A. A lot of them take the long road around. All the way over to Farmer and back again, which is close to a mile each way, so it's a good two-mile walk, which would take maybe half an hour or 45 minutes or up to an hour for a slow walker. Of course there's the multipurpose room here in Bolin that has dances and card games once in a while, and there's different activities going on. Lately there have been movies down there. There's been quite a few activities. I don't too much care for them myself, but quite a few of the women do, especially if they don't have too much company; it does take up their time.

Q. I think you mentioned the garden too?

A. Yes, you can walk over there now. I don't know whether they allow you in without an aide. You might have to have an aide with you. The time we went, we had an aide take us through it. It was very interesting.

Q. OK, I guess we've gone over all those places. Name some places in the hospital that a patient cannot spend time in.

A. Well, any of the old chronic buildings, like Jackson. I tried to get in there once to see one of the aides, and I got lost in there, and they don't actually allow you in there. Jackson and all. Actually, I've gone into Farmer just to look over it, but I don't know whether they do let you into the wards that you don't belong on. I imagine you could if you went visiting, but we were sort of nosying around. But the chronic wards, the old wards, they don't like you to go into.

Q. Why do you suppose they don't?

A. Well, probably it would be upsetting to the older folks. I know I just walked through one today, looking for an aide that works at Jackson but lives over here on the grounds. I wanted to talk with her, and I couldn't find her, and a lot of the doors were locked. But I know you're not supposed to be going into any of the doctors' offices or things like that.

Q. Why do you suppose you're not allowed to go into any of the doctors' offices?

A. Well, there's personal papers there and records and all. If you were invited there, if you have an appointment, it's different. But, of course, you're not supposed to be going around. The social workers and all the private offices here on the main floor are not open to. . . .

Q. Where else can you not spend your time?

A. I don't know. I know I've gone into Farmer and Green and been allowed to go there. I don't know. There haven't been too many places I've been that are off-boundaries.

Q. What do you do with most of your time?

A. Well, as I say, I spend 20 to 30 hours a week working for Mr. Rogers as his secretary. I also go to the small canteen when I'm back here. I go to cooking, which is down on the main floor here, and that's once a week. I go to art therapy, which is once a week in OT, and Mrs. Smith has charge of that. I also attend group therapy whenever I can. I'm not able to too much with Dr. Bly because I've been typing these lectures that Mr. Rogers has been giving to some of the people in the vicinity of this town. I've had to type the tape recordings of it and type it on a paper, so it's been an average of three hours a week, so I don't have too much time for anything else than spending it on the ward. Whenever I have time, I go to cooking or art therapy. I usually try to make art therapy—I like it very much.

Q. When you're in these other activities, do you know other people?

A. Oh yes, and if you don't know them you get to know them. Well, I've been here for over a year, and I've met many, many, many, many people.

Q. Do you know a lot of them on a basis where you can talk?

A. Yes, on a first name basis.

Q. When you go to the small canteen, do you visit sometimes?

A. Oh yes, if someone's sitting there that I know, I sit down and talk.

Q. Do you go out for walks sometimes?

A. Oh yes, especially when I was staying here weekends. Saturday morning I used to go for a walk.

Q. With someone usually?

A. With someone. We'd stop over at the large canteen. Several times we went bowling on Saturday morning.

Q. Usually the same friends that you would go with?

A. Well no, because a lot of them would be discharged, and you'd go with someone else.

Q. So you find no trouble in making new friends?

A. No.

Q. I see. Well, what are the places that you *must* spend time in?

A. Must?

Q. That you must, that's right.

A. On the wards. You're supposed to stay on the ward til 9. But I leave at 8:30 to go to work. If you have a logical reason to leave the ward . . . and then of course after 9 at night you have to be on the ward. Between 9 at night and 9 in the morning you have to be on the ward. From then on you can do as you will, as you wish.

Q. Taking as average or typical day, I'd like you to tell me what you do. What time do you get up?

A. Seven.

Q. You go directly to breakfast?

A. Yes, it gives me about one minute and a half to get dressed. I come back at 7:30 from breakfast, I do my ward duty. . . .

Q. That takes how long?

A. Well, depending on what you have to do. I have the windows to do, but I don't do those every day. I do a few and then neglect them for awhile and then I do a few more. Of course, keep the room clean too—I'm usually the one who mops the room because there are old people in the room and you couldn't ask them to mop it. So that takes until about 8:15, and I get changed, ready for work, put a dress on because I wear slacks around the ward all the time. I put a dress on and go to work. I get there about 8:45, and I leave there anywhere from 3 to 4. I have to be back at the ward around 4:30.

Q. And you probably eat lunch over there?

A. I eat at Johnson. I usually waste an hour . . . sit in the Johnson lobby and watch the people go by. And then I go back to work. Sometimes he needs me the whole day. Lately, now that the seminar is over with, he doesn't need me as much. I sometimes only go in for half a day. Like today—I only had to work half a day.

Q. Well, what is the usual length of time?

A. Usual? Well, for the past—from September up until now—it's been about 20 to 30 hours a week. Sometimes it's much less, maybe 15.

Q. So after lunch you keep going until about what time?

A. About 3 or so, and then I come back to the ward.

Q. Do you come directly back?

A. Usually, yes. I very seldom stop. You can stop at the large canteen and have coffee or something, but I have coffee on the ward, so I usually just come back and have a cup of coffee. I got into the habit of coming back then because I used to get medication at 4. Now I only get it twice a day, 8 in the morning and 8 at night.

Q. But you're still in the habit?

A. I still come back at 4, yes, or earlier. I can leave whenever the work is done . . . it doesn't matter. But sometimes, rather than come over here and do nothing, I'd just as soon sit there and answer the phone and fix the files and things.

Q. And then you stay on the ward?

A. I usually stay on the ward. By then the small canteen is closed, so I usually miss it, so I have instant coffee. I make myself a cup of coffee and stay on the ward until supper at 5.

Q. How long does that last?

A. About half an hour. And then go back to the ward. It's the longest time of the day.

Q. What do you generally do on the ward?

A. Watch television. I do a lot of reading. I have the *Reader's Digest* sent up here every month, and I have taken books from the library. And, later on, watch television. I do a lot of letter writing, and as I say, my husband comes three times a week, and neighbors and relatives come once a week, and my family comes once a week.

Q. When they come, do they usually come in the evening?

A. My husband comes in the evening, and so do the neighbors. The relatives and my mother and father, you can never tell. They come whenever they can. I very seldom go to any of the activities here. I used to when I first came here, but it gets to be old hat with you after a while.

Q. What time do you turn in for the day?

A. Anywhere from 9 to 10 to 11 on the weekends, when we're allowed to stay up late.

Q. How much visiting do you do in the hospital? I mean not visitors coming in but visiting friends here.

A. Not too much. One woman, especially close friend of mine who came in about the same time and had relatively the same reason for coming in that I did, is now up on locked ward, and I can't visit her. The girls that are on the other wards maybe I visit once a week—that were on my ward and then transferred to another ward for one reason or another. But usually most all the friends I do have are either on the ward or have been discharged.

Q. Well, how about some of these friends that you go for a walk with?

A. Yes, well, some of them are now, as I say, going home weekends; I don't have a chance to go for these walks.

Q. Do you have friends in other buildings?

A. Well, since they've had this change of buildings, whereas the town of Newclark is here in Bolin, New Salem is in Johnson, and Newbury is in Farmer, there are quite a few people that were in Bolin that have been transferred to these other buildings, and I have gone over to see them once in a while or seen them on the street walking. Sometimes I have gone over to Johnson to see some of the people who have been transferred. But you sort of lose contact with them after a couple of weeks.

Q. In your opinion, what is the hospital supposed to do for patients in general?

A. Well, set them out on the right road back to normalcy. Most of us that come in here are upset or depressed or have some mental disorder of one type or another. Actually, we must learn to live with our stresses and strains in the outside world, and the best way of learning to live with them is to be deprived of living with them for awhile, because you sort of glance back at what you've been doing and what has been bothering you and it helps you a great deal to be away from these stresses and strains. I think the hospital, the doctors and all help in this respect.

Q. What would you do if there wasn't a hospital?

A. Well, I don't know what I would have done in the beginning because I was . . . no one had referred me to a doctor. I had been having trouble, having thoughts, the wrong kind of thoughts, experiencing lack of sleep for over a month. And yet I couldn't find anyone that would help me. I didn't go to a psychiatrist, though. It never dawned on me—I thought it was all physical. So if there was no hospital, I probably would have had to go, or someone would've had to refer me to . . . for psychiatric treatment outside the hospital, with a psychiatrist. But I had gotten so bad that I think I would've needed hospitalization of some sort anyway. I probably would've gone to the Newclark Hospital.

Q. What are you supposed to do while you're in the hospital?

A. Rest. That's the main thing that I had to do. I was completely run-down, both physically and mentally, and I had to rest. And, of course, that's just about all I did was sit on my butt and rest, and it got pretty . . . pretty tiresome after a while.

Q. Is there anything else that you're supposed to do in the hospital?

A. Well, of course, follow instructions and directions, do what the doctor tells, and the nurses, aides . . . what you're supposed to do.

Q. How is that supposed to help, I mean, doing what they say?

A. Well, they seem to know the best method of helping us, and you have to pay attention or you're not going to be helped. I think a lot of it is up to you yourself. The doctors, the nurses, the aides, the psychologists, all can do just so much. But if you don't have the will, well the will to get better, I don't think you're going to get better. I know several cases of young women in here, younger than myself, some older, but I don't think they'll ever really be cured.

Q. Because they haven't the will?

A. I don't know if it's the will or maybe they have given up or maybe they just can't get back to reality, but they're so completely out of it, they don't want to face reality. They don't want to face their own life—they're just happy with the life in here.

Q. What are doctors for? How are they supposed to help you get better?

A. Well, of course, psychiatrists are regular doctors, and they take care of you, both physically and mentally. They really point out to you some of your problems or your anxieties, but they can't tell you exactly what they are. They sort of lead you to them and let you figure them out.

Q. What are psychologists for? How are they supposed to help?

A. Well, you got me there. I haven't the faintest idea. I think they just take up a lot of room. Knowing you're a psychologist. . . . But I guess they sit and talk to you and get you to start talking about yourself and all. . . . I've yet to know what they really do, because not one of them has ever told me anything constructive as far as my problems are concerned. I know several of them have gotten me to start thinking about the problem. I'd talked to them and then afterwards sort of rehashed what I'd told them and started thinking of things. But they don't say, "Now this is true. This, this, this and this is wrong with you, and you should correct yourself and do this, this, this and this, and then you'll be better."

Q. Is this what you're looking for?

A. That would be wonderful if you could, but it just doesn't happen that way.

Q. Well, what are nurses for? How are they supposed to help you?

A. Well, they are also for mostly physical problems. If you need anything, if you have a cold or are very underweight, or things like that, they'll help you with that. And, of course, if you're upset, they'll give you a good shot for yourself, calm you down, restrain you, put you in jackets if you need to— I've seen some of those.

Q. What about aides? How are they supposed to help you?

A. Like nurses mostly. They watch you, make sure you're not going to hurt yourself. You know, like a police agent in the hospital. And they're wonderful companions too, they're wonderful people. I've found a lot of aides who've really aided me.

Q. By being companions?

A. By being people. By understanding. There's a lot of them that have a real understanding of a person's problems, and just by . . . once in a while you hear them sitting down talking about their home life and the problems they have, and you sit down and realize, well, they're human, too, and they have just as many problems as you have. Yours just got the better of you, and you weren't on too wrong a track, and life goes on in spite of yourself.

Prevailing Conceptions
of Mental Illness:
The Search for a New Paradigm

Other than war itself, there is perhaps no human problem of such manifest significance that has remained so elusive as mental illness. Despite innumerable clinical observations recorded throughout history and thousands of empirical studies conducted within the last century, our understanding of mental illness is still tragically inchoate. The history of the study of mental illness is littered with the debris of discarded conceptions of psychosis as well as now abandoned methods of treatment. This gloomy history is too well known (Bellak, 1958; Deutsch, 1949; Joint Commission on Mental Illness and Health, 1961; Redlich and Freedman, 1966; Zilboorg and Henry, 1941) for us to have to recapitulate it here. Today, too, we have our conceptions of mental illness and our preferred modes of treatment; what we do not have is any assurance that our present views and procedures are any more enlightened and efficacious than those that we now consider out-moded. Indeed, there seems to be an increasingly uneasy feeling that we may be on the wrong track altogether, that our conception of mental illness is largely adventitious and accordingly fails to take into account its essential features. Scheff's (1966) recent statement epitomizes this sense of disquietude:

> Although the last five decades have seen a vast number of studies of functional mental disorder, there is as yet no substantial, verified body of knowledge in this area. At this writing there is no rigorous knowledge of the cause, cure, or even the symptoms of functional mental disorders. Such knowledge as there is, is clinical and intuitive, and thus not subject to verification by scientific methods. . . . Many investigators, not only in the field of schizophrenia, but from all the studies of functional mental disorder, apparently now agree not only have systematic studies failed to provide answers to the problem of causation, but there is considerable feeling that the problem itself has not been formulated correctly (pp. 7–9).

The noted historian of science, Thomas Kuhn, has suggested (1962) that when a consensually held paradigm (by which he means a shared understanding of the nature of a given phenomenon) comes to generate a growing skepticism concerning its adequacy and when new competing paradigms begin to appear, the stage is set for a scientific revolution—one of those discontinuous transformations of a science in which a phenomenon is fundamentally reconceptualized, thereby unleashing a burst of revitalizing research activity. It is our contention that we are currently witnessing the incipient phases of such a revolution in the field of psychopathology. In order to substantiate this view, we have to demonstrate the presence of the two conditions necessary for a scientific revolution: (1) the inadequacy of the existing paradigm and (2) the emergence of new paradigms.

This book grew out of certain initially unsystematic observations of the behavior of patients[1] in a large state mental hospital, observations which, as we shall attempt to make clear, we found increasingly difficult to reconcile with prevailing conceptions of mental illness. For example, it appeared to us that many patients were able to a surprising extent to control their hospital fate. For

---

[1]When we use the term *patient* or *mental patient* in this book, we refer almost exclusively to persons diagnosed as "schizophrenic."

the most part, they did not seem to be the hapless and acquiescent figures we had been led to expect. Indeed, rather than the
passive victims of institutional life, many of them seemed not only
highly motivated to govern their own activities but also extra-
ordinarily successful at doing so. What made these observations
so remarkable to us was not so much that these activities were
often in violation of the hospital's treatment program and therefore essentially subversive in character but also that they could
be carried out while most of the staff remained unaware of them
or failed to recognize their significance.

We would notice, for example, that many patients were quite
adept at managing their impressions (Goffman, 1959) in interactions with the staff so as to secure certain benefits that might
otherwise be unattainable. In addition to these episodic displays
of manipulativeness, we found that patients were able to establish
a comfortable hedonic life style in the hospital that was as anti-
thetical to staff desires as it was undetected or misinterpreted.
What we observed, in short, was that these mental patients were
acting in very much the same way normal members of any ordinary community would be expected to behave. At all events, they
were definitely *not* behaving like mental patients are "supposed"
to: they did not appear to us to be the disoriented, dependent,
and socially inept creatures that the textbooks described. On the
contrary, what struck us repeatedly and forcibly was the incon-
testable way in which the behavior of these patients, most of
whom had been classified as schizophrenic, resembled that of
ordinary human beings.

Our descriptive goal in this book is in fact to do nothing more
than to portray as faithfully as we can—without resorting to the
preconceived categories of psychiatric modes of thought—how the
mental patient behaves both within and outside of the hospital.
Our objective in furnishing this description, however, is by no
means purely an ethnographic one, a mere attempt to document
patients' way of life in one particular institution. Our objective,
rather, is to make it irrefutably clear that the dominant conception of mental illness does not permit one to account even for
the most mundane activities of mental patients and warrants
therefore being cast aside in favor of a more adequate paradigm.
It will be apparent that our aim is primarily revolutionary rather
than descriptive, a point that cannot be affirmed without our

sounding somewhat grandiose and perhaps a trifle absurd. In self-defense, we can say only that we were at first reluctant revolutionaries; ultimately, however, the compellingness of our observations exceeded our loyalty to the prevailing perspective, and we were quite unable to resist joining forces with some of those whose revolutionary views we shall illustrate later in this chapter. Before doing so, however, it is incumbent that, by examining its defining characteristics, we demonstrate the inability of the dominant conception of mental illness to handle the kind of observations and experimental findings that comprise the substantive body of this book.

DEFINING CHARACTERISTICS OF THE DOMINANT PSYCHIATRIC CONCEPTION OF SCHIZOPHRENIA

To speak of the "dominant psychiatric conception of schizophrenia" may seem to imply that there is a consensus among students of schizophrenia concerning how this variety of mental illness is to be described and understood. As Scheff (1966) has indicated, however, even a superficial survey of psychiatric opinion is sufficient to leave the reader dazzled and perplexed by the apparent diversity of constructs used in discussing the "nature," origins, and treatment of schizophrenia. In what meaningful sense, then, can one refer to the "dominant psychiatric conception of schizophrenia"?

In our view, the answer to this question depends on making a firm distinction between a *conception* of schizophrenia and a *theory* of schizophrenia. Once this distinction is made, it becomes obvious that a shared conception (that is, a paradigm) of a phenomenon need not generate a consensually held theory about that phenomenon. In academic psychology, for example, competing behavioristic theories of learning were for a long time able to flourish despite widespread agreement concerning how the phenomenon should be approached—a consensus that was particularly likely to be evident when such theories were challenged by the radically different assumptions of cognitively oriented theories. In psychiatric thinking about schizophrenia, too, we believe, there is a certain conceptual uniformity in the midst of appreciable theoretical heterogeneity. Our aim, accordingly, will not be to consider "theories" of schizophrenia (except in an incidental way) but rather to focus on what is central and common to psychiatric views of schizophrenia.

Although theories of schizophrenia as a whole are not notable for their explicitness, it is usually possible to identify without too much difficulty at least their major assumptions and propositions. The analysis of the psychiatric conception of schizophrenia, however, is a somewhat more difficult undertaking, for its essential features have to be extracted, as it were, rather than gleaned from casual examination. Formally, at any rate, a theory has (or is supposed to have) a certain structure among whose components are postulates and theorems; and foreknowledge of this underlying structure facilitates the analysis of any theory. It is not, however, so easy to specify the components of a *conception* or indeed even to be certain whether a structural approach is appropriate; one's mode of analysis is therefore more arbitrary and is more likely to be based largely on heuristic principles.

For our purposes, we have found it helpful to regard the psychiatric conception of schizophrenia as consisting of a series of axioms concerning the "nature" of the schizophrenic. These axioms are to this paradigm what mores are to a culture: widely shared, virtually self-evident propositions that are rarely challenged because they are, for the most part, maintained without awareness. We submit that this set of axioms may be viewed as constituting the *implicit belief system* of many of the most influential psychiatric students of schizophrenia, and it is this belief system we mean to scrutinize here.[2]

Possibly the primary axiom that underlies the psychiatric conception of the schizophrenic is that there is some fundamental and undeniable way in which he differs from the rest of mankind. More is implied here than that the schizophrenic is an extremely disoriented and forlorn individual defining the negative end of an adjustment continuum; he seems to be on another unnamable

[2]Although we characterize the psychiatric perspective as an *implicit* and therefore largely unstated belief system, occasionally, as in some of the quotations to be cited later in this chapter, its tenets are expressed in unmistakably *explicit* fashion.

and terrifying continuum altogether, one that ordinary men never encounter except perhaps in their dreams. He is supposed to inhabit an unreal world governed by fantastic images and a pervasive illogicality. It is almost as if he had defected from the human race to join another antediluvian one, for his schizophrenia renders him both other and less than human. He becomes, in Schooler and Parkel's (1966) phrase, "an alien creature."

> . . . the chronic schizophrenic is intriguing because he negates many criteria which have been used to distinguish men from other animals . . . the chronic schizophrenic is not Seneca's "reasoning animal" or Spinoza's "social animal," or even a reasonably efficient version of Cassirer's symbol-using animal, yet he manages to maintain, at least in the environment in which he is found, an apparent unshakeable equilibrium. Being truly the exception that proves the rule, he provides a unique vantage point from which to study the intricacies of human behavior. Since he violates so many functional definitions of man, there is heuristic value in studying him with an approach, like that which would be used to study any alien creature . . . (p. 67).

One of the consequences of taking such a view of the schizophrenic is that a special set of concepts has to be devised in order to describe and account for his behavior. This is of course a necessary and therefore predictable outgrowth of regarding the schizophrenic as not quite human, for, if he is not, the generally held principles of human behavior suddenly become inapplicable. So it is that a kind of theoretical double standard arises, with one set of explanatory principles for human behavior and another for schizophrenics. We shall return to this point later.

A second and related belief concerning the schizophrenic is that his "illness" represents the nadir of a disintegrative disease process that results in a profound impairment of virtually all psychic functioning. As Schooler and Parkel (1966) suggested, it is this deficit perhaps more than any other that sets the schizophrenic apart from the rest of us. Schizophrenia appears to involve a process of socialization in reverse in which the afflicted individual is progressively shorn of the qualities that stamp men as human, until finally nothing remains but, in Becker's (1964) terms, "a ludicrous caricature of cultural man." A representative description of this primitization process is provided by Arieti (1954):

> In the course of the illness, the patient gradually relinquishes common symbols and reverts to paleosymbols, that is to symbols which he himself creates and which have no consensual validation. The paleosymbols represent a return to the level of the autistic expression of the child. As it happens in children, however, these paleosymbolic expressions are not completely original and private, but use remnants of common symbols. . . . This process of desocialization and desymbolization is sometimes delayed or arrested by restitutive phenomena. With the progression of the schizophrenic process, however, the process of desocialization increasingly impoverishes the patient's repertory of common symbols. With the advancing impoverishment of common symbols it becomes progressively more difficult for the patient to assume his own role and to visualize the roles of others. This process reveals how much of man is actually made of social life. What was obtained from others is eliminated, man remains an insignificant residue of what he used to be (p. 482).

A third belief with which we shall be especially concerned in this book is a derivative of the second: The schizophrenic is regarded as an involuntary victim of his "illness," over which he has about as much control as he can exercise in the conduct of his personal life, that is, virtually none. Both intrapsychically and in his external affairs, then, the schizophrenic is conceived to be very much a person in whom and to whom *things happen;* he is, accordingly, almost completely unable to be a causal agent in determining his own fate. He is characterized as passive, dependent, acquiescent, and weak; in the pursuit of rational goals, he is hopelessly and pathetically ineffectual. Only in the realm of fantasy is the schizophrenic vouchsafed a certain, though limited, competence. There is, in the schizophrenic, Redlich and Freedman (1966) say,

> a concomitant loss of focus and coherence and a profound shift in the meaning and value of social relationships and goal directed behavior. This is evident in the inability realistically to implement future goals and present satisfactions; they are achieved magically

or through fantasy and delusion. . . . As the patient becomes deficient in discriminating his outer and inner reality, primitive, infantile, sexual, aggressive, and passive wishes, as well as fantasies and drives, gain prominence, surface to consciousness, and often appear uncontrolled (pp. 463–464).

Becker (1964), too, echoes Redlich and Freedman in stressing the schizophrenic's inability to control his own fate and functioning and his resultant withdrawal into subjectivity. He is, writes Becker,

> . . . inexorably caught in a formula of human failure; a formula for a complete breakdown in functioning, in which the grotesque fantasy-world crowds out all possibility of action and conscious control; a formula that leads to progressive withdrawal, from social to personal deterioration. . . . The schizophrenic, lacking behavior patterns, has no chance for manipulating means and ends (p. 71).

We view these three axioms as providing the common underpinning for theories of schizophrenia, and together they constitute the core of the present psychiatric paradigm of schizophrenia.

Now the observations of schizophrenic patients to which we alluded at the beginning of this chapter and which we shall document in the next three chapters obviously cause serious problems for the paradigm we have just adumbrated. Evidence of the purposeful and successful structuring of one's life in the hospital in a fashion consistent with his primary motivations on the part of the chronic schizophrenic patient is strikingly incongruous with the behavioral implications of the psychiatric paradigm. That chronic schizophrenics can engage effectively in the subtle artifices of impression management and can establish personally satisfying and quite rational styles of life within the hospital are simply not *derivable* consequences from the axioms we have enumerated. And here an instructive paradox arises. It goes without saying that we are far from the first to have observed that the behavior of schizophrenics is much of the time preeminently purposeful, coherent, and effective; that it is, in short, not distinguishably different from that of normal human beings. Many psychiatrists, too, in their off-duty moments must often recognize a pronounced strain of rationality in the behavior of their schizophrenic patients. Why, therefore, has this aspect of patients' behavior been not merely obscured by psychiatric analysis but also made to stand in obvious contravention to it?

THE ASSIMILATIVE FUNCTION
OF PARADIGMS

Historians of science (for example, Conant, 1947; Kuhn, 1962) have made it plain that counterinstances in themselves are not sufficient to cause a paradigm to be discarded. In part this is because what is legitimized as scientific fact is largely dictated by the paradigm itself, and all paradigms outlaw some observations that would be recognized by others. Kuhn indicates the usual fate of a contrary datum:

> Assimilating a new sort of fact demands a more than additive adjustment of theory, and until that adjustment is completed—until the scientist has learned to see nature in a different way—the new fact is not quite a scientific fact at all (p. 53).

All paradigms perform such assimilative functions for their adherents. The psychiatric paradigm pertaining to schizophrenia, however, is especially likely to regard as inadmissible any data that seem to imply that the schizophrenic is functioning in a way similar or superior to that of a normal human being. Ordinarily, such a result would be incompatible with the paradigm, and typically it is reinterpreted so as to appear consistent with the paradigm after all. A few examples will illumine this process of counterinstance reinterpretation.

In a study of role taking conducted by Helfand (1956), it was predicted that schizophrenics would show poorer role-taking ability than normals. To Helfand's surprise, however, the differences favored his schizophrenic subjects. Helfand interpreted these findings as follows:

> What is it that permits, or enables the schizophrenic to respond with such sensitivity? Secondly, why do they respond with such

sensitivity? . . . The behavior of the normal individual was to project a preconceived set of ideas based primarily on a commonly shared cultural stereotype (in the experimental situation). The patients, responding to the same information, made better use of it, although their reactions were highly idiosyncratic. Sarbin's description of the schizophrenic as lacking a "generalized other" concept seems appropriate to the results here. The schizophrenic, possibly because of this lack, responded to the cues as he perceived them. . . . The schizophrenics' . . . lack of a conventional frame of reference . . . served to contribute to their hyperacuity. . . . Assuming that schizophrenics lack this generalized other, such an impairment, with resultant hyperacuity, should be found in younger children, and in emotionally disturbed children as compared to well adjusted children of the same age (pp. 39–40).

In Helfand's interpretation, the unexpected superiority of his schizophrenic subjects in role-taking skills is "explained" as a result of a putative lack of a "generalized other." Seen now as a consequence of a psychological *deficit,* the schizophrenics' skills are transformed into a liability, and Helfand can conclude by comparing his subjects to emotionally disturbed children. The paradigm remains intact.

Grayson and Olinger (1957), confronted with the embarrassing findings that schizophrenics could simulate "normalcy" on the MMPI (Minnesota Multiphasic Personality Inventory) and that their ability to do so was correlated with briefer hospitalization, salvage the paradigm with this interpretation:

Perhaps a word of caution is in order lest the data lead to unduly optimistic interpretations of the changes observed in the "improved" cases. It might be well to distinguish between favorable prognosis for early discharge as against therapeutic accessibility. Many patients capable of simulating normalcy on a *lip service* basis might also be capable of producing *superficial changes* in their outward behavior which would enable them to be rated much improved and ready for release. Some of these patients may merely have gained *temporary control* of their erratic and frequently unmanageable impulses without any new basic understanding or mastery of their impulses (Italics ours; p. 77).

Here a patient's ability to manage his impressions and (inferentially, to be sure) control his fate is regarded as only a fleeting and insubstantial remnant of normal functioning. Eventually, what is essential in the patient's "nature" (his "unmanageable impulses") will reassert itself, causing him to revert to his former condition and revealing his normalcy to be a sham. (Of course, we do not deny that this may be a proper interpretation; our point is only that, if the paradigm is to be preserved, any apparently normal behavior must be recast so that it is indeed merely apparent and adventitious.)

Even "chronic" normalcy can be reevaluated so as to be congruent with an assumption of underlying pathology as this quote from Mowry (1964) will attest:

> Mental hospitals gradually accumulate in the continued treatment section a large number of chronic patients who appear refractory to the traditional forms of therapy, including tranquilizing medication. This population consists of some chronically disturbed patients, but the greatest number is *stabilized,* with or without tranquilizers, at a level compatible with open-ward care; they function on the hospital grounds without grossly overt behavior problems, and many manage adequately in the community on passes and short leaves. These patients are considered in fair *remission* from their illness and generally respond in acceptable ways to the usual interpersonal and social demands. Nevertheless, they reveal little or no motivation to live outside the hospital and are considered to have a strong institutional dependency. A part of this inertia is associated with a continuing but *covert mental illness;* however, a large share is contributed by the active acceptance of the sheltered life provided for these passive, dependent individuals by a publicly supported hospital . . . (Italics ours; Mowry, in Fairweather, 1964, p. v).[3]

No one, in our judgment, has argued more convincingly against the routine translation of a patient's normal-appearing behavior into paradigmatic psychiatric cant than the sociologist Erving Goffman (1961). We should like to conclude this section on the

[3] Not only does this excerpt demonstrate the vast assimilative powers of the psychiatric paradigm but also, as will be apparent later on, it is instructive in another way as well. Mowry's observations are highly consistent with many of those reported in this book; his interpretations, however, are antipodal to ours. Such a state of affairs makes it evident that we are dealing here with a clash between paradigms, not between "facts." "Facts" enter in only insofar as their recognition and significance are influenced by the paradigm in question.

assimilative function of paradigms by quoting at some length Goffman's incisive commentary on the consequences of indiscriminate use of the psychiatric perspective.

> The patient's presence in the hospital is taken as *prima facie* evidence that he is mentally ill, since the hospitalization of these persons is what an institution is for. A very common answer to a patient who claims he is sane is the statement: "If you aren't sick, you wouldn't be in the hospital." . . . Since the current conduct of the patient is supposed to be a profound reflection or sign of his personality organization—his psychic-system—any sudden, apparently unprovoked, alteration in either a "healthy" or a "sick" direction must somehow be accounted for. Sudden changes for the worse are sometimes called relapses or regressions. Sudden changes for the better are sometimes called spontaneous remissions. Through the power of these words the staff can claim that, although they may not know what caused the change, the change can be handled within the medical perspective. Of course, this interpretation of the situation precludes one's employing a social perspective. In what is called sudden regression, the new conduct may involve no more or less illness or health than any other alignment to life; and what is accepted as spontaneous remission may be a result of the patient's not having been sick in the first place. I am suggesting that the nature of the patient's nature is redefined so that, in effect if not by intention, the patient becomes the kind of object upon which a psychiatric service can be performed. . . . An overall title is given to the pathology, such as schizophrenia, psychopathic personality, etc., and this provides a new view of the patient's "essential" character. When pressed, of course, some staff will allow that these syndrome titles are vague and doubtful, employed only to comply with hospital census regulations. But in practice these categories become magical ways of making a single unity out of the nature of the patient—an entity that is subject to psychiatric servicing. Through all of this, of course, the areas of "normal" functioning in the patient can be discounted and disattended, except in so far as they lead the patient willingly to accept his treatment (pp. 379–380).

THE SEARCH FOR A NEW PARADIGM

"Once it has achieved the status of a paradigm," writes Kuhn, "a scientific theory is declared invalid only if an alternate candidate is available to take its place. No process yet disclosed by the historical study of scientific development at all resembles the methodological stereotype of falsification by direct comparison with nature. . . . The decision to reject one paradigm is always simultaneously the decision to accept another . . ." (p. 77). Scientific revolutions, then, do not occur merely because a paradigm is revealed to be seriously flawed; another paradigm must stand ready to replace it. In the present context the question now becomes "Do we currently have an alternate paradigm for schizophrenia that will allow us to come to terms with the facets of the behavior of schizophrenic patients that prove an embarrassment to the psychiatric perspective?"

We have already said that at the outset of our work we had no revolutionary intent—we were not interested in helping to overthrow one system of thought in order to supplant it with another. Our purpose was principally to discover how patients spent their time in a state mental hospital; our task, then, was in the main descriptive and theoretical. The observations we referred to earlier (see page 29), however, forced us to examine closely the tenets of the psychiatric perspective simply and only because, as we have said, the behavior of patients made that perspective appear distressingly inadequate as a basis for understanding what we were witnessing. We hope we have made it clear that it was not merely that the psychiatric perspective was irrelevant to the kind of data we were collecting; we found instead that this paradigm either obscured the significance of some of these data or, if we were to take them seriously, either failed to predict them or predicted their opposite. To retain the psychiatric perspective in the face of such overwhelmingly contrary data appeared to us to be more than fatuous: It was an impossibility. Only drastically different assumptions about the "nature" of the mental patient would, we felt, permit us to make sense of our observations and experimental findings.

Gradually the outlines of what we have here called a paradigm began to crystalize. We found that, rather than regarding the schizophrenic as a qualitatively dissimilar being from the rest of us, the assumption most congruent with our data was to emphasize just how human he was. Instead of viewing his "illness" as the manifestation of some sort of recondite disease process, it appeared to us that it represented his not-altogether-irrational attempt to cope with the problems he confronted in his everyday life; to call it a "disease" seems, as we shall indicate later, merely to reflect a value judgment and retards understanding of the schizophrenic's behavior by invoking a specious, albeit widely accepted, analogy with pathological physical processes. Finally, what appeared most blatantly erroneous to us in the psychiatric conception of the schizophrenic was his portrayal as a weak, acquiescent, and ineffectual individual. Everything that we saw pointed to exactly the opposite characterization: The schizophrenics we observed were, as a rule, manipulative and resourceful individuals whose behavior was calculated to serve their primary motivations, which they were able to satisfy with surprising frequency and ease. Paradigms transform reality, and the schizophrenics we studied and that we describe in this book bear almost no resemblance to those depicted in standard psychiatric accounts. In a word, ours appear to have all the characteristics of ordinary human beings.

Just as we were by no means the first to record the kind of observations detailed in this book, we are not enunciating a totally new paradigm. Within the past decade views similar to ours have been propounded only to languish in obscurity or, if they were noted, to be quickly dismissed as, in effect, heretical. Scientific revolutions, however, in contrast to political ones, are never accomplished quickly, and repeated assaults upon a dominant paradigm are usually necessary before it begins to give way. To demonstrate that there are others who endorse the revolutionary paradigm we have outlined (though perhaps such a demonstration is really unnecessary), consider the independently elaborated views of Rakusin and Fierman (1963), whose conception of the schizophrenic is virtually point-by-point identical to ours:

> The chronically psychotic patient is human, not sub-human or different in quality from the people treating and managing him. No matter how bizarre his behavior, the patient is still capable of discriminating external events, including the presence of other humans.
>
> His behavior is purposeful, reactive, motivated, and goal directed. . . .
>
> The patient has personal interests, and purpose, pursues them avidly, and is distracted from them only with difficulty.
>
> We explicitly assert our belief that the patient is human, and

qualitatively not different from ourselves, in order to take issue with "evidence" that he is somehow sub-human. . . . Our view of psychosis constitutes more a "way of life" hypothesis than a "disease" hypothesis. We assume the patient to have what he regards as good reasons for behaving the way he does—that he has in mind some purpose from which his behavior logically follows (p. 140).

The seemingly neglected work of Artiss and others (1959) also supports our contention that the schizophrenic's behavior is purposeful and is designed to get personally satisfactory outcomes from his environment. Symptoms and other deviant behavior may therefore represent a kind of tactical device that schizophrenics use to manipulate their interpersonal environment in order to attain certain goals:

> The data have demonstrated that certain schizophrenic trainee soldiers engage in a symptomatic statement, "I am weak and ineffectual," for which the anticipated reply is, "all right then, we'll release you from your obligations—and from our group." . . . Did the young schizophrenic patients in this group behave in symptomatic ways in direct anticipation of release from the group, as part of a total goal-directed plan, as it were? We believe that the data will answer this question in the affirmative . . . (p. 19).

Of course, the most vigorous and well-known spokesman for the new paradigm is Thomas Szasz, whose writings (1958, 1961, 1963, 1965) have earned him a reputation as a polemicist of the first rank. In his most celebrated book, *The Myth of Mental Illness* (1961), whose title leaves no doubt about his revolutionary aspirations, Szasz demolished the commonly maintained assumption that the psychiatric conception of mental illness represents merely an objective and dispassionate account of psychopathology. Several years earlier, however, Szasz had already enunciated his position with characteristic elan:

> More precisely, according to the common sense definition, mental health is the ability to play whatever the game of social living might consist of and play it well. Conversely, to refuse to play, or to play badly, means that the person is mentally ill. The question now may be raised as to what are the differences, if any, between social non-conformity (or deviation) and mental illness. Leaving technical psychiatric consideration aside for the moment, I

shall argue that the difference between these two notions—as expressed for example by the statements "He is wrong" and "He is mentally ill"—does not necessarily lie in any observable facts to which they point, but may consist only of a difference in our attitudes toward our subject. If we take him seriously, consider him to have human rights and dignities, and look upon him as more or less our equal—we then speak of disagreements, deviations, fights, crimes, perhaps even treason. Should we feel, however, that we cannot communicate with him, that he is somehow "basically" different from us, we shall then be inclined to consider him no longer as an equal but rather as an inferior (rarely, superior) person; and we then speak of him as being crazy, mentally ill, insane, psychotic, immature and so forth (p. 188).[4]

Sarbin (for example, 1964, 1967a, 1967b, 1967c, 1967d, 1967e), employing the techniques of linguistic, logical, and historical analysis, has attacked the concept of mental illness with vigor. Concerning schizophrenia, Sarbin (1967b) states:

The readiness to accept the concept of schizophrenia as a disease entity is perhaps the most widespread social implication of the continued uncritical reliance on the mental illness (and mental health) myths. To explode the myth one needs to present arguments to show the lack of utility of the major concepts contained within the myth, e.g. schizophrenia, hallucinations, anxiety. Support for the official structure of knowledge may be undermined when its metaphorical roots are exposed. . . . I have also argued that the concept of schizophrenia has negative utility for scientists and professionals concerned with the management and welfare of disordered persons. (In this context, I define disordered persons as those who engage in improper, silly, unpopular, perturbing, embarrassing, perplexing, or eccentric conduct, i.e., *conduct that violates propriety norms*) [Italics ours]. . . . A number of observations render questionable the continued use of the disease concept: (a) the fact that the label is currently attached to an infinite variety

[4]Arieti's (1959) rebuttal is curiously flaccid: "Szasz's is probably one of the strongest attacks ever made on the Kraepelinian concept of dementia praecox (schizophrenia). Although I admit that in what we call the schizophrenic syndrome there is much that is indefinite, variable, inconstant and accessory, I *feel* [italics ours] nevertheless that there is a more or less homogeneous core which recognizes the schizophrenic person as such and leads us to some conclusions, some of which have pragmatic value. The fact that the nature of this core has not been fully or uncontroversially determined points to the incompleteness of the concept of schizophrenia but does not prove it is a fallacy" (p. 501).

of behaviors; (b) that professionals cannot agree on whether or not the label should be applied to a particular person; (c) that similar behaviors in certain classes of persons are not so labeled; and (d) most important, that the label unwittingly may be used to designate profound effects of legal, police, medical, and nursing practices on the conduct of the disordered person. Notwithstanding, the weight of tradition and the bureaucratization of the legal and medical institution that give service to disordered persons continue the employment of the concept of schizophrenia (pp. 359–360)

. . . While I may be charged with unrestrained hyperbole, the historical facts are undeniable. The same culture thought model that generated the medieval demoniacal model also produced the modern mental-illness model to explain conduct that does not meet rule-following prescriptions. The rejection of such an entrenched thought model by the relevant professionals is in the nature of a scientific revolution (1967a, p. 454).

Other writers (for example, Goffman, 1961; Haley, 1965; Laing, 1967; Levenson and Gallagher, 1964; Ludwig and Farrell, 1966, 1967; Mowrer, 1960; Scheff, 1966; Towbin, 1966) could be cited who advocate (at least aspects of) the paradigm we are proposing here. However, the point that we wanted to establish is, we think, sufficiently buttressed by those whose views we have already quoted: We conclude that a new paradigm does exist, that it has won the adherence of a number of observers, and that, therefore, the time is ripe for a scientific revolution.

CONCLUSION: THE CASE FOR A PARADIGMATIC REVOLUTION

Our purpose in this chapter has been to show that the conditions necessary for a scientific revolution—inadequacy of the existing paradigm and availability of at least one alternate paradigm—are present in the domain of concern to us in this book, schizophrenia. If the analysis offered in the preceding pages is substantially correct, the *desirability* of such a revolution is apparent. Nevertheless, a number of reasons favoring a paradigmatic shift of the kind we advocate have not always been explicitly indicated and, in concluding, it may be well to spell these out.

The first of the reasons is simple and rests on the principle of parsimony. The current psychiatric perspective requires that a special set of assumptions and concepts be applied to the individuals it classifies as psychotic; the principles governing the behavior of the rest of us are apparently either not relevant or sufficient where psychotics are concerned. The new paradigm obviates the need for special principles and seeks to understand the behavior of *all* persons in terms of a common body of propositions.

The second advantage of the new paradigm is a heuristic one. A new conception of the schizophrenic, while obviously not depriving us of any previous sound and hard-won knowledge, opens our eyes to hitherto unsuspected possibilities and sets the stage for creative theoretical and research innovations. When led by a new paradigm, Kuhn (1962) says, "It is rather as if the professional community had been suddenly transported to another planet where familiar objects are seen in a different light and are joined by unfamiliar ones as well (p. 110)."

Another advantage that, though important, we need not dwell upon, has to do with the explanatory power of the new paradigm. We have already suggested that the psychiatric perspective tends to obfuscate many aspects of the behavior of schizophrenic patients by providing pseudoanswers to misconstrued questions. The data presented in the next three chapters of this book will provide the basis for an even more serious indictment of the psychiatric perspective: As we have mentioned, many of the findings are flatly at variance with predictions that could be derived from this implicit belief system. Although the reader must decide for himself, of course, how compelling the new paradigm is, the fact that (for us) it evolved in the course of our research insures a substantial fit between much (but not, in any logically entailed way, all) of our data and our paradigm.

Finally, we come to a question that has remained close to the surface of much of the discussion in this chapter, the question of values. We think we can take it for granted, without having to argue the point, that there are few investigators who still seriously maintain the view that the study of schizophrenia utilizes only value-free constructs. One's very conception of schizophrenia, and not merely one's treatment procedures, is bound to be indissolubly linked to the values one holds about men and their behavior. Accordingly, we should like to express here an explicit and we hope not gratuitous value judgment: In our opinion, the psychiatric perspective has not only impeded our scientific understanding of the schizophrenic but also has resulted both in his being demeaned and therapeutically mismanaged. The consequences of even such an innocuous feature of the psychiatric approach as psychiatric classification can be far-reaching as well as unjust. We share the views of Goffman (1961), Szasz (1961), and others who deplore the unintended but potent psychic brutalities that an unenlightened psychiatric paradigm makes inevitable. The new paradigm holds out the hope that, however one chooses to "treat" the schizophrenic, he will not be deprived of his essential humanity.

To argue in behalf of a new paradigm for the scientific study of schizophrenia on admittedly nonscientific grounds may seem like a stark inconsistency. The first three factors, it may be contended, are legitimate criteria for the evaluation of any paradigm; but to endorse a paradigm on the basis of the values it implies is clearly inadmissible. Our answer to this objection is simple: To be maintained, any paradigm has to satisfy the canons of science, but there are always nonscientific reasons for supporting it as well. Such factors may not in themselves be *sufficient* to induce support, but neither can they nor should they be disregarded.

In urging consideration of a new paradigm for schizophrenia, we have attempted to enunciate our position in bold, forthright, and distinctly hortatory language. It is not the custom, after all, for those who espouse revolutionary causes to speak in muted phrases or to mince their words. A polemical style, of course, is not always the most effective device to convince skeptics, but we place greater reliance on our data than in our style to accomplish that task. Our purpose in expressing our views in this fashion was, rather, primarily to achieve a certain clarity in exposition—a clarity that is enhanced through the effects of sharp contrast and unqualified assertion. Such a course becomes irresistible when one recalls the words of our foremost contemporary aphorist, Eric Hoffer, who has written (1954): "It is impossible to think clearly in understatements. Thought is a process of exaggeration. The refusal to exaggerate is not infrequently an alibi for the disinclination to think or praise."

PLAN OF THE BOOK

It remains only to give some indication of the material contained in the subsequent chapters. The next three chapters comprise the substantive portion of this book. In Chapter 2, we shall be concerned with the manipulative tactics of mental patients. In experimental or quasiexperimental settings, we focus on patients' use of impression management as a means by which they achieve outcomes congruent with their primary motivations. In Chapter 3, we explore the continuity between patients' in-experimental behavior and their ways of adapting to their everyday hospital environment. Of particular interest here are the styles of life that patients evolve in the institution, patterns of activities that demonstrate unmistakably the extent to which patients are able to conduct their own lives so as to satisfy the needs most important to them. Chapter 4 deals with another kind of continuity: the continuity between the patients' life style outside the hospital community and what they develop within the hospital community itself. It will be apparent that these three chapters are sequenced so that an ever-increasing segment of a patient's activities are available for scrutiny: In Chapter 2, he is presented in experimental situations only; in Chapter 3, the setting is his everyday hospital milieu; finally, in Chapter 4, he is examined as he shifts between his hospital and outside community.

In the last two chapters, we consider the implications of our work. In Chapter 5, after an integrative summary of the research findings presented in the three preceding chapters, we return to many of the issues raised in this introductory chapter, which are then discussed in light of the new evidence. We also suggest some further research studies to determine the generality of our findings. Chapter 6 is taken up with the "treatment" procedures that seem indicated if the new paradigm for schizophrenia is accepted. In this chapter, we propose a series of recommendations, radically at variance in their implications with current policy, governing the establishment and operation of special communities for patients.

Experimental Studies
of the Manipulative Tactics
# of Mental Patients

So long as he remains hospitalized, the mental patient appears to suffer from a severe power disadvantage. In terms of formal power that may be exercised over him, he finds that his life, down to the most trifling aspects, can be controlled by his keepers, the hospital staff. Goffman (1961) has described in numbing detail the extraordinary range of activities for which a patient must ask staff permission before he can engage in them. There are, in addition, matters about which, even though they may and often do profoundly affect a patient's fate, he does not have even an acknowledged right to express his own opinion and have it seriously considered. A patient's life inside the hospital, then, would seem to be governed almost totally by staff decisions. According to this view, a mental patient is a person whose right of choice has been formally preempted by others.

This description, though it is not inaccurate as far as it goes, is nevertheless fallaciously incomplete, for it ignores altogether the element of the patient's counterpower. In Chapter 1 we argued that, as a rule, the mental patient is not a passive and helpless victim who abjectly acquiesces to the enormous power that any "total institution" (Goffman, 1961) has the authority to wield.[5] We see him, rather as a person who, within the limits of his situation, is concerned with living his life as he deems fit, just as any ordinary person of any other functioning community would be. We would expect, therefore, that a patient would attempt to control his own fate as much as possible; even when an unwelcome one is unavoidable imposed, we would anticipate that he would attempt to escape it or, that failing, resist it. If these efforts to counteract the power of the staff are at all successful, it means that the latter's control over the patient is neither so formidable nor implacable as our initial analysis implied. We are suggesting, in short, that the power of the staff can be mitigated to a considerable extent through the application of counterpower by the patients.

It is important to be clear about the nature of the power that is available to staff and patients. The power of the staff is *legitimate* power, exercised in accordance with the hospital's professed and actual standards governing the treatment and management of its residents. It is, therefore, power that is backed by the machinery of publicly constituted authority. The power that the patients can exploit and with which we are principally concerned here is fundamentally *subversive* in character. By subversive we, of course, do not mean that the patients seek to overthrow the power system, but rather that they undermine it by violating it in ways that are often not obvious or even visible to the staff. As Goffman (1959, 1961) has convincingly shown through numerous examples, a patient may indeed appear to acknowledge and even honor the power system while actually in subtle and deliberate fashion mocking the staff who enforce it as well as the system

[5] Not all mental patients, of course, dwell in hospital settings that qualify as "total institutions." Nevertheless, it is frequently assumed that almost regardless of the structure and climate of the institution, it still functions as the primary determinant of the patient's in-hospital behavior (Downing, 1958; Fairweather, 1964; Goffman, 1961; Gordon and Groth, 1961; Stanton and Schwartz, 1964).

itself. (This device clearly represents a morale-boosting symbolic "turning of the tables" with little personal risk, because it involves a patient's private joke on the staff.) All of this implies that although the *form* of patient counterpower is conditioned by the legitimate power system, it acts insidiously to subvert that system.[6] The "balance of power" within a mental hospital, then, is a balance between the formal, sanctioned power of the staff and the covert, illegitimate power of the patients.

IMPRESSION MANAGEMENT AS A FORM OF PATIENT COUNTERPOWER

The manifestations of patient counterpower are surely legion, and many of them have been carefully delineated by several observers (Artiss, 1959; Goffman, 1961; Scheff, 1966; Szasz, 1961; Towbin, 1966). In the three experimental studies to be reported here, however, we focus on one general and widely used manipulative tactic that Goffman (1959) has called "impression-management." By this term Goffman means only that we can and generally do manage our expressive behavior so as to control the impressions that others form of us. Through selective disclosure of some information (it may be false information) consistent with the character we mean to sustain for the purpose of an interaction, coupled with suppression of information incompatible with that projection of self, we establish a certain definition of ourselves that we attempt to maintain throughout the interaction episode. In simple and posssibly misleading terms, we act, we play roles. As a technique of interpersonal manipulation, it ought to be exploited by patients for the same reasons we use it—one can often increase the chances of achieving desirable outcomes from others by appearing to be a certain sort of person. Indeed, one may suggest that, if anything, mental patients should be even more inclined to use this tactic than we are because (1) their objective situation makes them more dependent on others for good outcomes, and (2)

[6]To allay possible misinterpretations, it should be stated that we do not mean to suggest either that the power exercised by patients is primarily symbolic in expression or that it represents only a reaction against the legitimate power enjoyed by the staff.

they are either in fact or normatively prevented from attaining the outcomes by more direct means (for example, by simply requesting permission to be allowed to go home for the weekend).

Now, the notion that mental patients can employ impression management in the service of their own motivations would be a point hardly worth mentioning, let alone emphasizing, were it not for the prevailing view that schizophrenics are for the most part incapable of executing such highly "socialized" interpersonal gestures. This mode of interaction certainly collides at any rate with the stereotype of the chronic schizophrenic as regressed and unresponsive to others. We propose, on the contrary, that not only is the mental patient capable of impression management but that also he uses it surprisingly successfully, perhaps in part because of the expectation of others that he cannot dissemble at all (or at least not without their being aware of it). If one is ready to grant at the outset that mental patients, like ordinary mortals, can manipulate and deceive for their own ends, the findings to be presented will come as no surprise. If, however, one is unaccustomed to viewing patients in this way, their experimentally induced behavior will occasion a distinct and perhaps a rude shock.

Impression management, like any other manipulative tactic, is given form by the actor's motivations and goals. It becomes necessary, therefore, in order to predict how a patient will present himself, to specify the motivations and goals that characterize him while in the hospital. Although direct evidence will be presented only in later chapters, for the time being we shall simply assert as an hypothesis that the predominant motivations of the majority of the chronic patients at any rate center around remaining in the hospital and being able to enjoy life as much as possible there. If this is so, we would expect, for at least this class of patients, that they would present themselves in such a way as to safeguard their current status. This would imply, for example, that they should be reluctant to criticize openly hospital policies and that they should try to give the impression that they are still "sick" enough not to merit discharge, but not "sick" enough to warrant being assigned to a closed ward. The typical patient, then, is assumed to be primarily motivated by a desire "not to rock the boat" and to preserve his style of life within the hospital. The form of his impression management can accordingly be anticipated to reflect these motivations.

IMPRESSION MANAGEMENT THROUGH INGRATIATION

Jones (1964) has suggested that *ingratiation* may be regarded as an illicit interpersonal tactic that can be used to secure benefits (or to avoid harm) from others. Jones maintains that ingratiation is illicit because it takes place within a normative framework that it appears to honor but in fact does not. Ingratiation is said to involve an attempt to increase one's attractiveness to others who have the power to reward or punish the individual; in this way, the ingratiator, if he is successful, can increase the likelihood of achieving good outcomes (or avoiding bad ones). Ingratiation, finally, may take many forms: one may flatter the target person, agree with his opinions, present oneself in an engagingly modest way, and so on.

Especially important for our purposes are the conditions under which ingratiation is likely to occur. According to Jones, they comprise a state of affairs where the potential ingratiator (1) wants some benefit, x (or wants to avoid some harm, z), (2) is dependent on somebody else, o, to provide it, and (3) believes that some action on his part will induce o to provide x (or to refrain from performing z). Presumably, a tactic that would be classified as ingratiating by an external observer (though not necessarily labeled so by the performing individual) will occur when the norms relevant to the situation preclude other more legitimate means (for example, a simple request) or when, in any case, an ingratiating maneuver promises the best or perhaps the only chance for success.

It is not difficult to see that these conditions are very often present for the mental patient. Our analysis of his power position in the hospital suggested both his dependence on others and his likely recourse to illegitimate forms of power, of which ingratiation is an obvious example, to achieve his goals. Furthermore, because ingratiation involves presenting oneself in such a way as to influence the impression others form of him, it clearly represents one instance of behavior in the service of impression management. All these considerations point to an empirically verifiable assertion: Mental patients can be expected to manage their impressions, through the use of ingratiation tactics, in their interactions with the staff. The following study, by providing patients with an opportunity to engage in ingratiation through flattery, permits a test of this hypothesis.

METHOD

For this study (conducted by B. Braginsky, D. Ridley, D. Braginsky, and K. Ring), a thirty-item test, labeled "Hospital Opinion Inventory," was constructed. The items that were to be answered using a true-false format were of three types: (1) eleven items that expressed highly implausible but positive opinions about the mental hospital (for example, "There is nothing about the hospital that needs improvement of any kind," "Without exception, every single nurse and aide in the hospital is as good to patients as a mother or father would be to their child"); (2) nine realistic but mildly critical opinions about the hospital (for example, "There are times when I wish the hospital treated me better," "There are times when I feel that some of the hospital staff do not quite understand me"); and (3) ten unrealistically critical opinions about the hospital (for example, "The hospital always takes advantage of patients," "There is not a single good thing about being a patient in this hospital").[7]

It seems reasonable, in view of the content of these items, to assume that patients who tend to agree with the first type and disagree with the second type are expressing exaggeratedly and unrealistically positive opinions about their institution. No mental hospital with which we are familiar comes close to meriting such encomiums. Whether such hyperbole can be taken as indicative of ingratiation or some other factor(s) plainly depends on the nature of the test-taking instructions, which are considered next.

Two experimental conditions, which differed in the instructions Ss received concerning the test, were created. In the *Public* condition, Ss were told:

> We are here today to find out how you feel about the hospital. We are interested in your opinions. On this test you will find statements which measure how you feel about this hospital. We would like you to answer them as accurately as possible. Please sign your

[7]The entire inventory may be found in Appendix A.

name on the top of the first page. This is important because some of the hospital staff will review these tests later and they would like to know which patients filled out which tests. That is, they will want to identify who took the tests. This can only be done if you sign your name. Thank you.

In the *Anonymous* condition, Ss received this induction:

We are here today to find out how you feel about the hospital. We are interested in your opinions. On this test you will find statements which measure how you feel about this hospital. We would like you to answer them as accurately as possible. Please do not sign your name to the tests. We are not interested in who takes the test. All we are interested in is how patients, as a group, feel about the hospital. So remember, do not sign your name. Thank you.

It will be obvious that of the two statements, Ss in the *Public* condition ought to be the more highly instigated to ingratiate themselves if our assumptions about their motivations (see p. 52) are sound. Only they as individuals have something to lose through endorsement of opinions critical of the hospital; only they as individuals stand to gain by praising the hospital and its staff. Ss in this condition, therefore, have a twofold motivation to ingratiate themselves: to avoid arousing the censure of the staff (prompting disagreement with the critical items) and to increase the likelihood of continued favorable treatment (prompting agreement with the positive items). Because they individually can receive neither credit for the approved response nor blame for disapproved ones, Ss in the *Anonymous* condition should show considerably less evidence of a desire to ingratiate themselves.[8]

SUBJECTS   Sixty-five male and 45 female open-ward patients served as Ss in this study. Ss were drawn from four male wards and three female wards, all of which were similar in patient characteristics such as age, education, length of hospitalization, and diagnostic category. The mean age of the patients was 43.2 years with a standard deviation of 14.1. The mean education level of the sample was 10.5 years with a standard deviation of 4.6. Their median length of hospitalization was 3.7 years. In terms

[8]The rationale for including unrealistically critical items is not germane to the present argument and will be outlined later.

56 EXPERIMENTAL STUDIES

of general diagnostic categories, 82 percent of the sample had
been diagnosed as schizophrenic, 3 percent had been labeled as
psychotic but not schizophrenic, and the remainder had been
judged nonpsychotic. A comparison of males and females within
each experimental condition failed to disclose any significant
differences on these demographic variables.

Each experimental condition was composed of patients from
two male wards and one and a half female wards. The wards were
tested in groups in order to keep the patients from feeling that
they had been singled out and thereby to reduce any anxiety that
such an interpretation might have aroused. In addition, this procedure was adopted to make the anonymous induction more
credible as well as to convey the impression that the patients were
involved in a hospital opinion survey rather than an experiment.

EXPERIMENTAL DESIGN   Ss were classified according to
sex and the experimental instructions they had received, thus
giving us a simple two-by-two factorial design. The number of
Ss in each of the conditions was unequal and ranged from 22 to
35.

RESULTS AND DISCUSSION

Table 1 presents the mean number of items answered in an ingratiating direction. It is clear that, as expected, Ss in the *Public*

TABLE 1

*Mean Number of Ingratiating Test
Responses According to Experimental
Condition and Sex*

SEX	EXPERIMENTAL CONDITION	
	PUBLIC	ANONYMOUS
Males	10.23 ($N = 35$)	7.97 ($N = 30$)
Females	11.36 ($N = 22$)	6.30 ($N = 23$)

condition more often respond to the test items in an ingratiating fashion ($F = 21.30$, $p < .001$). Neither the main effect for sex nor the interaction was significant, and, of course, neither was anticipated to be. Furthermore, within sex comparisons using the Newman-Keuls procedure (Winer, 1962) show a significant experimental condition effect for both males ($p < .05$) and females ($p < .01$). Finally, no significant relationships were found to exist between any of the demographic variables mentioned earlier (see p. 55) and test scores.

Ten unrealistically critical items had been incorporated into the test in order to evaluate the possibility that low ingratiation scores reflected not simply realistically critical appraisals of the hospital but instead obviously unwarranted, negativistic ones. Because we found a low absolute incidence of endorsement of such items in both conditions (means of 1.91 and 2.06 for the *Public* and *Anonymous* conditions, respectively), this interpretation is effectively ruled out. Low ingratiation scores are not indicative of hypercritical attitudes toward the hospital.

In one sense the findings of this experiment are not at all remarkable—patients express more flattering (indeed absurdly flattering) opinions about their institution and its staff when their responses can be traced. If a professor reported that midway through the semester his students evaluated his course more positively when they signed their names on the evaluation form then when they did not, we would probably not jump out of our seats with astonishment. Yet we have merely documented the analogous finding for mental patients. The reader is entitled, therefore, to his "so what?"

In our view, what makes these findings noteworthy is, paradoxically, that they are so banal—imagine, mental patients respond just like anyone else! They, too, seem capable of ingratiation. This is not surprising at all perhaps until one recalls the kind of assertion mentioned in Chapter 1 that avers, for example, that schizophrenics are so different from the rest of us that they should be studied as if they were "alien creatures."

Now, it may be objected that we have not demonstrated conclusively that the clear experimental condition effect we obtained is a function of ingratiation or that, in any case, the results are at all illuminated by making reference to the construct of impression management. We agree that it would be rash to make the claim on the sole basis of the data from this study. Although some alternative interpretations can be excluded (for example, one cannot contend that the patients in the *Public* condition simply wanted to please the staff without reference to possible future self-benefit because that motivation should have been just as strong for Ss in the *Anonymous* condition), it is always possible in principle at least to suggest other parsimonious explanations. In addition, the evidence (Jones, 1964) against an ingratiator perceiving his behavior in those terms is so strong that even had we endeavored to inquire into Ss' interpretation of their own behavior or its motivation, we probably would not have been able to make a convincing case for our point of view. It seems only reasonable, then, to conclude that the data from the present experiment are consistent with the ingratiation hypothesis and with the assumption that mental patients can engage in impression management, but that there may be other interpretations of the data just as compelling.

Suppose, however, we continue to entertain our interpretation as a reasonable possibility in order to generate further research that may eventually allow us to place greater confidence in it. Viewed in this light, the data suggest that patients are quite capable of acting in their own self-interest, at least to the extent of misrepresenting their own opinions about the goodness of the hospital and its staff. We had been led to expect this outcome because we had some other evidence (still to be adduced) that made us believe that many patients were motivated to remain in the hospital, ostensibly because the life they were able to lead inside was preferred over alternatives available outside. That is, these patients appeared to us to stay in the hospital not so much because their pathology required them to, but primarily because they voluntarily chose to do so. If this assumption is correct, it would have some important implications for the kind of impressions a patient could be expected to foster.

A patient cannot remain in a mental hospital simply because he likes it (or likes it better than his available alternatives); he has to justify his being there. The justification for residing in a mental hospital is that one is mentally ill. The inference is inescapable, and even an "alien creature" such as a "mental patient" could be expected to be able to deduce it.

If patients will misrepresent their opinions concerning the mental hospital *because* of the reasons we have proposed, then they should be motivated to misrepresent their mental condition as well. If they want to remain in the hospital, they had better convince the staff that they are "sick." The next study gave them the chance.

CONTROLLING ONE'S HOSPITAL FATE THROUGH IMPRESSION MANAGEMENT

In an experiment carried out by B. Braginsky, M. Grosse, and K. Ring (1966), we selected two classes of patients to participate who we felt (on the basis of data to be presented in Chapter 4) ought to differ substantially in their motivation to remain in the hospital. We expected that Newcomers (patients who had been hospitalized less than three months and for the first time) would be, as a group, primarily motivated to leave the hospital whereas the Old-timers (those who had been there three months or longer —the majority for over three years) would prefer to remain. We do know that as a group, Newcomers have the highest discharge rate in the hospital (80 percent are released within the first three months) while Old-timers have the lowest (only 17 percent are discharged during any one year). There are, of course, many factors which contribute to this difference, and we do not wish to deny that the nature and degree of psychopathology is one of them. What we do want to emphasize, however, is that to a very considerable extent this difference in discharge rates may perhaps be attributable to nothing more esoteric than a patient's desire to stay in or leave the hospital and his ability, through impression management, to achieve his particular goal. That, at least, was the hypothesis with which we began.

METHOD

In this experiment we again employed a test-taking procedure, constructing for this purpose a so-called mental status test. This test consisted of 30 MMPI items all of which had received relatively neutral ratings on a social desirability scale (Dahlstrom and Walsh, 1960).[9] We selected only such items in order to maximize the effect of the experimental manipulations, to be described later, on Ss' test responses.

Two forms of the test, differing *only* in the title printed on the test booklet, were then prepared. One version was called the "Mental Illness Test" while the other was labeled the "Self-insight Test." The items, of course, were identical.

Two experimental conditions, each using one form of the test, were next established as follows:

In the *mental illness* test condition, Ss were told, prior to taking the test:

> This test is designed to measure how severely mentally ill a patient is. We have found that the more items answered True by a patient the more severely ill a patient is and the greater are his chances of remaining in the hospital for a long period of time. Patients who answer many of the items False are less severely mentally ill and will probably remain in the hospital for a short period of time. We would like to find out how ill you are.

In the *self-insight* test condition, Ss heard these instructions:

> This test is designed to measure how much knowledge a patient has about himself. We have found that the more items answered True by a patient the more he knows about himself, the less severely ill he is and the greater are his chances of remaining in the hospital for a short period of time. Patients who answer many of the items as False know less about themselves, are more mentally ill and will probably remain in the hospital for a long period of time. We would like to find out how much you know about yourself.

It is apparent that we have deliberately provided Ss with a "script," as it were, for managing their impressions, if they desire to do so. In effect, we tell a patient that if he wants to be adjudged as mentally ill and thus deserving to remain in the hospital, he should respond True to most of the items when he takes the mental illness test, but for the most part False when the test presumably deals with self-insight. What this means, of course, is that, if patients do indeed engage in impression management,

[9]The entire test may be found in Appendix A.

they are forced in taking one test to admit that they have the very symptoms they deny when taking the other. Conversely, if one wants to be regarded as less mentally ill, he must in general answer False to the items of the mental illness test and True to those of the self-insight test. It should be pointed out that if, instead of attempting to present himself in a particular way (that is, either as mentally ill or mentally healthy) a patient responds to the test items in terms principally of his psychopathology, he should answer the test items very much the same way, regardless of both the test title and the instructions he has received.

In addition to the two experimental treatments just described, one control condition was run. Here Ss received one or the other form of the test, but without the instructions that specified the appropriate "script." In this way, it was possible to examine the effect of the test titles alone in order to see whether they themselves were sufficient to bias patients' responses to the test.

SUBJECTS   All 60 Ss in this study were hospitalized open-ward male patients, classified as either Newcomers or Old-timers according to the criteria mentioned earlier (see p. 59). The mean age of the patients was 37.2 with a standard deviation of 10.6. Their mean educational level, according to years in school, was 10.2, with a standard deviation of 3.6. Not surprisingly, there were differences between the groups on both of these variables, with the Newcomers on the average younger (mean age, 31.3) and better educated (mean years of schooling, 11.0) than the Old-timers (mean age 40.0, mean years of schooling, 9.2). Diagnostically, however, there were no differences between Newcomers and Old-timers; 68 percent of all patients had been classified as schizophrenic, another 20 percent as psychotic but not schizophrenic, and the remainder were labeled neurotic. Within subject classes, there were no significant differences between conditions on any of these demographic variables.

Ss were run individually, and all were led to believe, not that they were participating in a psychological experiment, but rather that they were being given a standard clinical evaluation.

EXPERIMENTAL DESIGN AND HYPOTHESIS   Twenty Newcomers were assigned randomly and in equal numbers to the two experimental conditions; a like number of Old-timers were also allocated to each experimental condition. Because of the relative scarcity of Newcomers, only Old-timers were run in the control condition; again 20 Ss took part, divided into two equal groups. The experimental design may be summarized, then, as a two-by-three independent groups design with equal Ns.

The hypothesis under examination pertains just to the two experimental conditions and leads us to anticipate a statistical interaction of the following form: Newcomers should tend to answer False to the mental illness test but True to the self-insight test (thus conveying, so they believe, an impression of mental health), while just the opposite pattern should hold for Old-timers, (who, of course, believe that by so responding they will be regarded as mentally ill).

RESULTS AND DISCUSSION

The number of True responses for each of the three conditions is presented in Table 2. As can be seen, the predicated interaction

TABLE 2

Mean Number of True Test Responses
According to Treatment Condition
and Status of Patient

PATIENT STATUS	CONDITION	
	MENTAL ILLNESS TEST	SELF-INSIGHT TEST
Newcomers	13.00	18.80
Old-timers	18.80	9.70
Old-timers (control)	14.60	14.30

Source: Braginsky, Grosse, and Ring (1966).

emerges clearly: The modal response by the Newcomers is False to the mental illness test and True to the self-insight test; the reverse is true for the Old-timers. This interaction is highly significant ($F = 15.61$, $p < .001$). Moreover, within each subject

class, the difference between experimental conditions is significant ($p < .01$ for both Newcomers and Old-timers, using the
Newman-Keuls procedure). Thus, the overall impression that
Newcomers create by their test responses is one of considerable
mental health, despite the fact that in order to do so, one set of
patients must affirm symptoms that another set of comparable
patients disavows.[10] Similarly, Old-timers convey an impression
of mental illness by their (inconsistent) pattern of test responses.
These findings are, furthermore, precisely what one would expect
according to our initial contention that Newcomers are by and
large motivated by a desire to leave the hospital, Old-timers, by
a desire to remain, and that both classes of patients are quite
capable of managing their behavior so as to influence the kind
of decision made about them.

Examination of the control group means makes it evident that
the test labels in themselves do not systematically bias an S's
responses; a "script" in the form of a specification of the meaning
and consequences of test responses appears to be necessary to
produce the effect observed in the experimental conditions. A
comparison of Old-timers in the experimental and control conditions reveals a near-significant interaction ($p < .10$), the form of
which is clearly due to the marked divergence of the experimental
group means. This effect, though only of marginal significance, is
another indication of the extent to which patients can be induced
to present themselves as more mentally ill than they otherwise
might, as long as they know what responses will foster that impression.

We have interpreted the data from the present study as reflec-
tive of a patient's (1) desire either to leave or remain in the
hospital and (2) his ability to convey either an impression of
health or illness so as to (3) maximize the chances of realizing
his desires. There is another cogent interpretation, however, that
handles the findings just as easily and that therefore deserves to
be considered. Perhaps it is simply that chronic patients are more
likely to be more severely ill than newly arrived ones or, at least,
believe themselves to be. Rather than responding in terms of
putative motivations, then, it may be their conception of them-

[10]The ideal design for this type of study would require that each S be
used as his own control; the technical problems posed by this procedure,
however, made the present design more feasible.

selves, as influenced by their underlying pathology, that is affecting their test performance. A similar argument would be tenable for Newcomers.

Two points need to be made concerning this alternative interpretation before referring to data that bear on it. First, we are not asserting that it is a patient's pathology in itself that influences his test responses, for, if that were so, Old-timers, as we suggested on p. 61, would be expected to score higher (that is, give more True responses) under *both* test inductions. This interpretation holds, rather, that a patient's self-conception is, in part, determined by his pathology and that his test behavior reflects that self-conception. The second point is implied in what we have just said: A patient would still be regarded as having engaged in impression management, but for different reasons from those we have proposed. Instead of a patient's stay-or-leave motivations being relevant here, we would merely have to invoke a tendency to portray oneself in a way consistent with one's self-concept.

The only difficulty with this line of reasoning is that from the results of other studies (for example, Joint Commission on Mental Illness and Health, 1961; Levinson, 1964) most mental patients do not appear to think of themselves as mentally ill. Furthermore, some opinion-survey data of our own (to be presented in detail in Chapter 4) based on 189 hospitalized patients confirm these findings: 78 percent of our sample agreed with the item "Most patients in a state mental hospital are not mentally ill." And particularly pertinent to the alternative interpretation under consideration here is the fact that agreement with this item is uncorrelated with the length of hospitalization ($r = -.11$). In short, the available evidence fails to support the view that Old-timers are more likely to think of themselves (or at least other mental patients) as mentally ill.

Assuming, then, that the findings of the present study can most plausibly be regarded as pointing to the operation of impression management tactics on the part of our Ss, a question of crucial significance for our theoretical position suddenly looms prominent: If patients do indeed use impression management in an effort to control their own fate, precisely how successful are they in doing so?

Our view, of course, has been that in the main patients are not content to leave decisions affecting their welfare entirely in the hands of others, but attempt through the use of whatever counterpower tactics that are available to them to insure that their situation in the hospital is at least moderately tolerable if not downright enjoyable. We have suggested, furthermore, that the manifestations of patient counterpower are likely to be covert, subtle, and normatively illicit and that one form that such counterpower would take is that of impression management. The question we are asking, therefore, is "Is such counterpower not only effective in principle, but effective in fact in allowing a patient to achieve his aims while in the hospital?" Let us briefly review the evidence presented thus far.

The ingratiation study demonstrated only that patients will, under circumstances where it is likely to pay off, ingratiate themselves; there was, however, no evidence from that experiment that such ingratiation did indeed lead to desirable outcomes. The experiment we have just finished recounting offered only indirect support for the efficacy of impression management tactics—there was an association, at any rate, between imputed motivation to stay in or leave the hospital and discharge rates, a relationship for which we assumed impression management was the mediating variable. That interpretation is outlined in Table 3.

TABLE 3

*The (Hypothetical) Role of Impression
Management in Mediating Discharge
Rates for Two Classes of Mental
Patients*

PATIENT CLASS	ASCRIBED MOTIVATION	APPROPRIATE IMPRESSION TO BE FOSTERED	TYPICAL DISCHARGE DECISION
Newcomers	I want to leave	I am mentally healthy	Discharged
Old-timers	I want to stay	I am mentally ill	Retained

However intriguing this interpretation may appear to be, no one could make a convincing case for the causal efficacy of impression management on the basis of the data that suggested it—there are too many other explanations.[11] What we plainly need is evidence that shows in clear and unmistakable fashion that a patient's impression management can directly influence his fate in the desired way. The following experiment was designed with just this objective in mind.

EFFECTIVENESS OF IMPRESSION MANAGEMENT AS A COUNTER-POWER TACTIC

In the two studies already reported, patients were afforded an opportunity to manage their impressions via performance on an impersonal, paper-and-pencil test. In the experiment about to be described (B. Braginsky and D. Braginsky, 1968), we fashioned a more stringent and less artificial situation in which to test the efficacy of impression management tactics; specifically, our procedure involved requiring a patient to submit to a clinical interview conducted by a staff psychologist. Not only is such a face-to face encounter more representative of the usual conditions under which impression management occurs but also, for mental patients particularly, this kind of evaluative interview setting is one with which they are familiar and which, because of the decisions presumably based on such interviews, ought to enlist strong motivations to engage in impression management in the service of their own personal goals.

METHOD

Thirty male patients living on open wards were advised two days prior to the experiment that they had been scheduled for an interview with a staff psychologist. Although each patient was to be interviewed individually, all 30 were brought simultaneously to a waiting room. After each patient had been interviewed, he

---

[11]For example, perhaps patients with a greater desire to leave the hospital do in fact make faster progress in dealing with their emotional problems, perhaps they are more likely to take part in formal treatment programs, perhaps the psychiatric staff is biased in favor of discharging younger persons (more likely to be Newcomers) more rapidly than older ones, and so on.

was not allowed to return to this room. This was done in order to prevent the patients who had completed their interviews from communicating anything about them to those who had not.

Each patient was escorted to the interview room by an assistant who casually informed the patient in a confidential tone about the purpose of the interview. According to a random procedure, patients were actually given one of three alleged purposes that constituted the independent variable of the study. The interviewer was unaware of the conditions to which Ss had been assigned, thereby eliminating interviewer bias. The three inductions were as follows: In the *Discharge* condition, patients were told, "I think the person you are going to see is interested in examining patients to see whether they might be ready for discharge." Patients in the *Open Ward* condition were informed, "I think that the person you are going to see is interested in examining patients to see whether they should be on open or closed wards."[12] Patients assigned to the *Mental Status* condition were told, "I think the person you are going to see is interested in how you are feeling and getting along in the hospital."[13]

After greeting each patient, the interviewer asked, "How are you feeling?" If a patient responded with a description of physical symptoms only, he was asked, "How do you feel mentally?" If, on the other hand, he dwelt exclusively on his mental state, he was asked, "How are you feeling physically?" All responses were tape-recorded. At the end of two minutes,[14] the interview

[12]It may appear as if this would not be a credible induction because no patient enjoying open-ward status would believe that he could be put on a closed ward on the basis of the forthcoming interview alone. At the time this experiment was conducted, however, the hospital was in the process of a major reorganization, and the question of possible changes in one's ward status was a salient one.

[13]Mental status evaluation interviews are typically counducted yearly. Patients who have been in the hospital more than a year (as had all of ours—see following) expect, therefore, to be interviewed for the purpose of determining their residency status.

[14]Obviously, psychiatrists would never base such important decisions as, for example, being discharged, on a two-minute interview. Nevertheless, in order to provide an opportunity for impression management that might *influence* such decisions, two minutes was more than sufficient. Data to be presented later indicate in any case that even so brief a sample of a patient's behavior as these interviews provide is adequate to afford a basis for reliable judgments by psychiatrists. It is interesting to note, incidentally, that the typical mental status interview conducted by these psychiatrists is rarely longer than half an hour and that, according to Scheff (1966), the average in-court psychiatric interview is only about ten minutes long.

was terminated and the real purpose of the experiment disclosed.

Three staff psychiatrists from the same hospital independently rated each of the 30 tape-recorded interviews during two 40-minute sessions. These psychiatrists had no prior knowledge of the experiment and were unfamiliar with the patients. They were told by E only that Ss were mental patients residing in the hospital and that as a group they represented a wide range of diagnostic categories.

The psychiatrists rated the patients on the following dimensions: (1) the patient's degree of psychopathology, using a five-point scale ranging from "not at all ill," scored as 1, to "extremely ill," scored as 5; (2) the amount of hospital control a patient needed, ranging on an eight-point scale from complete freedom ("discharge"), scored as 1, to maximum control ("closed ward–continual observation"), scored as 8; and (3) the structural or qualitative aspects of a patient's speech, such as pressure of speech, affect, volume, and so on. The score for each patient's speech characteristics was based on the sum of the psychiatrists' ratings of 14 Lorr scale items (Lorr, 1953). Each item was rated on an eight-point scale ranging from "not at all atypical" (1) to "extremely atypical" (8) verbal behavior.

SUBJECTS   All 30 male Ss were long-term (more than two continuous years of hospitalization) schizophrenics living on open wards who were randomly selected from ward rosters to participate in this experiment. Their mean age was 47.4 years, with a standard deviation of 8.4. The mean educational level of the sample was 8.0 years of schooling, with a standard deviation of 3.4. Their median length of hospitalization was ten years. Forty-three percent of the sample had been diagnosed as chronic, undifferentiated schizophrenics, 37 percent as paranoid schizophrenics, 10 percent as catatonic, and 10 percent as simple schizophrenics. There were no differences between the three experimental conditions on any of the aforementioned variables.

EXPERIMENTAL DESIGN AND HYPOTHESIS   The design of the present experiment is that of a simple one-way factorial with three treatments. Ten Ss were allocated to each condition.

Our experimental hypothesis is once again predicated on motivational considerations. We assume, first of all, that because all our Ss are schizophrenic Old-timers, they, as a group, should be motivated to remain in the hospital. We assume also, however, that they want to retain the privileges of open-ward living. Because a rational strategy to achieve the former goal would seem to be to present oneself as "mentally ill" (and thus justify one's continuing to reside in the hospital) while to achieve the latter would entail that one appear moderately healthy (and thereby justify one's current ward status), we may make the following prediction: Ss in the *Discharge* condition ought to represent themselves as more mentally ill than a comparable set of Ss in the *Open Ward* condition. The test of this hypothesis and of the effectiveness of the expected mode of their impression management will be provided, of course, by the psychiatrists' ratings. Because mental status interviews are generally used to evaluate a patient's suitability for discharge, we would expect that Ss in this condition would be similar in their mode of self-representation to Ss in the *Discharge* condition. In summary, then, our predictions arrayed in terms of increasing indications, through self-presentation, of mental illness may be expressed as follows:

$$OW < D = MS$$

RESULTS AND DISCUSSION

The mean interpsychiatrist reliabilities for the three variables rated were .89 for psychopathology, .74 for need for hospital control, and .65 for normality of speech characteristics—all satisfactorily high for our present purposes.

The mean ratings for the first two variables, psychopathology and hospital control, are given in Table 4. Both sets of ratings

TABLE 4

Mean Psychiatric Ratings of Patients' Psychopathology and Need for Hospital Control According to Experimental Conditions

	OW	D	MS
Psychopathology*	2.63	3.70	3.66
Hospital control†	2.83	4.20	4.10

*Range 1–5   †Range 1–8
Source: Braginsky and Braginsky (1967).

show very much the same pattern of differences—precisely the pattern, in fact, that was predicted. Both variables are affected significantly by experimental treatments ($F = 9.38$, $p < .01$ for psychopathology; $F = 3.85$, $p < .05$ for hospital control) and individual comparisons for both variables disclose that the mean for the *Open Ward* condition is significantly lower than the other two ($p < .01$ for psychopathology, $p < .05$ for hospital control), which in turn are not significantly different from one another. In short, these analyses make it clear that patients in the *Open Ward* condition appear significantly less mentally ill and in less need of hospital control than patients in either the *Discharge* or *Mental Status* conditions. Obviously, the patients in these conditions are quite successful in conveying distinctly different impressions of their psychological well-being to psychiatrists despite the fact that there is no evidence of any systematic variation in psychopathology across the three conditions.

In order to ascertain the means by which patients were able to effect these different impressions, we examined three fairly obvious manipulative tactics that patients might be expected to employ (not necessarily successfully, of course). They were (1) positive self-references, (2) negative self-references, and (3) normality of speech patterns. Indexes for the first two tactics were obtained by simple counting; the counts were made by three judges independently with a mean reliability of .95. The third index was based on the psychiatrist's ratings on the 14 Lorr scale items; a score for each S was obtained by summing the ratings over the 14 items.

The first two tactics, while seemingly lacking in subtlety, were nevertheless potent determinants of psychiatrists' judgments. The more positive self-references made by a patient, the less ill he was perceived to be ($r = -.58$, $p < .01$) and the less in need of hospital control ($r = -.41$, $p < .05$). Conversely, the more negative self-references emitted by a patient, the more ill he was perceived to be ($r = .53$, $p < .01$) and the more his judged need for hospital control ($r = .37$, $p < .05$). Congruent with our hypothesis that these patients are indeed capable of the fine art of impression management is the correlation of $-.55$ ($p < .01$) between positive and negative self-references, indicating, of course, that a patient's self-presentation tends to be internally consistent—those who make positive statements about themselves tend not to make negative ones and vice versa.

When self-references are compared by condition, we find—as we would now expect—that Ss in the *Open Ward* condition presented themselves in a significantly more positive manner than Ss in either of the other conditions. Only two patients in the *Open Ward* condition reported having any physical or mental problems, whereas 13 patients in the *Discharge* and *Mental Status* conditions made such complaints ($x^2 = 5.40$, $p < .05$).

The sheer frequency of positive or negative self-referent statements, of course, may not necessarily account for some important qualitative aspects of the impressions patients create. One patient may, for instance, indicate a single symptom but it may be a serious one (for example, hallucinations) while another may recount several trivial ailments. In order to provide a more sensitive measure of the treatment effects, therefore, all severe psychopathological symptoms (namely, reports of hallucinations or bizarre delusions) were tallied for each patient. A comparison of conditions revealed that not a single S in the *Open Ward* condition expressed such symptoms while nine Ss in the remaining conditions (that is, nearly half) did so ($x^2 = 4.46$, $p < .05$). Both in terms of number and severity of symptoms spontaneously mentioned, then, patients in the *Discharge* and *Mental Status* conditions present themselves as more mentally ill.

Concerning the last manipulative tactic to be analyzed, normality of speech patterns, no significant condition differences were found.[15] That there was a curtailed range of scores on this variable is indicated by the fact that 80 percent of the patients were judged to have relatively normal speech characteristics. Nevertheless, and consistent with our findings, there was a significant negative correlation ($r = -.35$, $p < .05$) across conditions between number of positive self-references and abnormality of

[15]The failure to find evidence of differential speech disturbance among the three conditions tends to cast doubt on the possible, though somewhat implausible, alternative interpretation that Ss in the *Discharge* and *Mental Status* conditions were made more anxious by the prospect of being discharged than were *Open Ward* Ss threatened with transfer to a closed ward. If this had been so, one could easily account for Ss in the former two conditions appearing more mentally ill—they were more upset. Although our speech disturbance data do not conclusively eliminate this interpretation, they render it even more unlikely.

speech patterns; that is, Ss whose speech was more disturbed tended to make fewer positive self-references. If anything, this concatenation of stylistic and contentual components in a patient's behavior ought to strengthen a judge's belief that the patient is mentally ill.

Altogether the results of this study strongly confirm our hypothesis as well as the set of assumptions on which it was predicated. It is clear that patients can and do act in interpersonal settings in such a way as to maximize the chances of satisfying the motivations we have attributed to them. Redlich and Freedman's (1966) assertion that the mental patient suffers from an "inability to implement future goals and present satisfactions" and that he achieves them "magically or through fantasy and delusion" would appear to stand in need of important qualification. When the self-interest of patients is at stake, they can present themselves *convincingly* as either "sick" or "healthy" depending on which mode of self-presentation is believed to increase the probability of desired outcomes.

Now, it is perfectly true that it is possible that psychiatrists might be misled and successfully deceived by patients when their evaluation is based on only a two-minute interview that is further restricted by providing psychiatrist-raters with just auditory cues. It is conceivable that actual face-to-face interaction for a longer period of time with the psychiatrist who is actually going to make important decisions concerning a patient's fate may sharply reduce a patient's ability to "con" the psychiatrist. That, we emphasize, is a possibility. Our research suggests, however, that it may instead be merely a vanity. It is equally conceivable to us at least that a patient who could fool a psychiatrist for two minutes could fool him for 30. Perhaps a patient is cleverer and a psychiatrist more fallible than we are accustomed to believe. This is no place, however, either for speculation or snideness. We need more research to settle the point, and the studies to be presented in the next chapter will help us to do so.

CONCLUSIONS

In this chapter we have argued that because of the nature and extent of an institutionalized mental patient's power disadvantage, he can be expected to exert counterpower that is mainly covert and subtle in form but surprisingly powerful in effect. This expectation itself is derived, of course, from the particular beliefs we hold about the sort of motivations and abilities most mental patients can be assumed to possess. These beliefs were outlined in Chapter 1, and we have no need to give more than the gist of them here: Mental patients, for all their pathology, are in most respects, most of the time, just like the rest of us; they want to live in a mental hospital in the same way that ordinary persons want to live in their own community—that is, they can be expected to try to satisfy their needs and, to a considerable extent, to be able to do so. But because a mental hospital, while a community of persons, is not just any community but one of a very special and potentially restrictive kind, the patient's attempts to control his own fate will often have to involve devious and indirect tactics. In this way, then, we were led to examine patients' use of one such tactic, that of impression management and several of its manifestations.

The data assembled from three separate experimental studies make it quite plain, we think, that patients do employ this tactic when given an opportunity (and one suspects that they often create their own opportunities for purposeful self-displays), that they do so with considerable skill, even finesse, and (as the third experiment demonstrated) with perhaps surprising effectiveness. It may be that any one of the reported experimental findings can be accounted for by some other factor(s) than impression management and the motivational variables we have postulated to underlie it; we doubt, however, that there is any other *single* alternative explanation that provides as satisfying and cogent an interpretation for all the data presented, considered collectively.

In each of the experiments described in this chapter, patients were placed in situations that were designed to arouse motivations leading to impression management and that furthermore often required that their impression management assume a certain modality (for example, self-presentation via a particular pattern of test responses). The question can be raised, however, whether in the absence of such experimentally induced conditions, patients would give the kind of performances observed in these studies. The answer would seem to depend on the extent to which there is a continuity between the motivations elicited in these experiments and those that govern the behavior of patients in their everyday hospital activities and interactions. There is already some reason to infer such a continuity inasmuch as our experimental settings were of course not represented as such, but rather as test or interview situations. Nevertheless, it seems important to document directly patients' hedonistic motivations that were implied, but not demonstrated, by our experiments and, once this is accomplished, to establish their consequences for patients' everyday behavior.

We turn next, then, to an examination of patients' behavior in the hospital at large in order to depict more fully the *styles* of *adaptation* that were so strongly suggested in our quasi-experimental settings.

Studies of Patient Styles
of Adaptation
to the Mental Institution

Although the life of mental patients in institutional settings has received, in this decade, considerable attention from social scientists, both the theory and research have been limited primarily to the nature of the hospital as a power agency and how its power shapes the patient's life. For the most part, this literature reflects the commonly held assumptions that patients, when confronted by institutional demands, are impotent and powerless (Goffman, 1961) or that they are basically inadequate, frightened, and acquiescent people (for example, Stanton and Schwartz, 1954; Fairweather, 1964; Gordon and Groth, 1961; Downing, 1958). Thus, individual differences are ignored, and the hospital, benign or oppressive, emerges as the prime determinant of the patient's institutional life.

We assume, however, that most mental patients, with the exception of those who are sensorily confused, have particular desired ways of living their lives as well as the ability to manipulate their environment in order to fulfill these desired life styles. Furthermore, there is no reason to believe that these desired ways of living (styles of adaptation) are terminated with the onset of hospitalization. The implication here is that neither the hospital nor the patient's psychopathology is the sole or even the major determinant of the patient's style of adaptation. Our point of view, therefore, generates a portrait of life in the mental hospital to which we have already alluded in the preceding chapters, namely, that mental patients appear somewhat hedonic both in their attitudes and behavior in the hospital and that their adaptation may in fact be counter to the espoused purposes and principles of the institution. In simple terms, we feel that mental patients want to and do enjoy in their own particular way their stay in the hospital, whereas the hospital administration and staff want the patient to engage in therapy programs so that they may be made well enough to be discharged. Our notions do not seem untenable, especially because supportive evidence has been accumulating (Levinson and Gallagher, 1964; Scheff, 1966; Artiss, 1958) and because we have already demonstrated in somewhat limited settings that mental patients can effectively employ counterpower strategies in an effort to control their fate.

STYLE OF ADAPTATION MODEL

In keeping with our beliefs that (1) mental patients follow the same laws of behavior as people in general and (2) the mental hospital, like any other community, offers a number of alternative modes of adaptation to its incoming members (see Levinson and Gallagher, 1964, pp. 50–51), a familiar model will be used in our inquiry of patient adaptation.

This model assumes that (1) the needs, attitudes, goals and interests that a person has at the time of entry into a new environment, as well as his previously learned techniques for adaptation, determine (2) where and how he will spend time in the new environment (that is, his *style of adaptation*), which, in turn, influences among other things, (3) what he learns about his new milieu, how long he will remain a resident there, and

```
┌─────────────────────────────┐
│  Antecedent Variables       │
│                             │
│  Needs, interests,          │
│  attitudes, skills at       │
│  adaptation, and so on      │
└─────────────────────────────┘
              │
              ▼
┌─────────────────────────────────┐
│  Mediating Variables            │
│                                 │
│  ADAPTATION STYLE               │
│         │                       │
│    Referents                    │
│         ▼                       │
│  Where P spends time in         │
│  community; what P does; how    │
│  much time he spends at         │
│  activities, and so on          │
└─────────────────────────────────┘
              │
              ▼
┌─────────────────────────────┐
│  Consequence Variables      │
│                             │
│  Information about          │
│  community, length          │
│  of residency, visibility   │
│  to community members,      │
│  and so on                  │
└─────────────────────────────┘
```

how visible he is to other members. To take a homely example, the avid golfer who moves to a new community would very likely seek out and spend as much time as possible at the local golf course. As a result, he would acquire a great deal of information about the golf course, its associated events, and its members. Conversely, this mode of adaptation would lead him to acquire little or no information about the libraries or pool rooms in his neighborhood. Moreover, there would be little chance for people outside of the golf course to get to know him. Another consequence would be that, if our golfer finds his golf course particularly satisfying, he would tend to remain a resident in that community rather than to move to a new one with less desirable facilities.

More specifically, with respect to mental patients, it is assumed that, prior to their entry into the mental hospital, they had developed and maintained a style of adaptation that they found maximally congruent with their needs, attitudes, and goals. Once in the hospital, they would be expected to spend a great deal of their time in the places in the hospital that would be most relevant to the satisfaction of these same motivations, needs, attitudes, and goals. In turn, their particular styles of adaptation would determine the kind of information they would acquire about the hospital, their length of stay in the hospital, and their visibility to certain persons in the hospital.

Thus, a hedonically oriented person upon entrance into the hospital would be expected to establish a hedonic life style there (for example, spend most of his time in the recreational areas of the hospital). One outcome of this way of life would be the acquisition of a considerable amount of information about the residential aspects of the hospital and a minimal degree of knowledge about the hospital staff and therapeutic facilities. In addition, if he spent most of his waking hours in the pursuit of pleasure, the psychiatry staff more than likely would be unfamiliar with him. On the other hand, a therapeutically oriented person would be expected to adapt to the hospital in a way that would allow for extensive contact with the hospital staff (that is, spend most of his time in therapy programs). This mode of adaptation should lead to the acquisition of more information about the staff and therapy programs than about the residential aspects of the hospital. He would also be a familiar person to the hospital staff.

We assume also that particular modes of adaptation either facilitate or hinder discharge from the hospital. For example, the hedonically oriented patient, spending most of his times in areas of the hospital that preclude staff contact (either because of a patient's purposeful avoidance or because of his greater interest in other areas) would have a greater chance of remaining in the hospital than the patient who spends most of his time interacting with the hospital staff.

One empirical approach to determine the validity of these assumptions is to ascertain (1) if mental patients differ in the kinds of adaptation styles they establish in the hospital and (2) if these styles of adaptation are determined primarily by the interaction between the patient's longstanding motivational system and the hospital environment rather than by patient psychopathology or institutional demands. A less direct, but a more pragmatic, first approach to this problem would be to determine whether patients differ with respect to certain assumed antecedents and consequences of styles of adaptation to the hospital. If patients do differ on these variables and if we find that this variation is neither logically nor empirically related to variation in patient psychopathology and institutional demands, inferential evidence would thereby be provided for our viewpoint. This, in fact, was the basis of the study conducted by B. Braginsky, J. Holzberg, L. Finison, and K. Ring (1967).

CORRELATES OF THE MENTAL PATIENT'S ACQUISITION OF HOSPITAL INFORMATION

Our discussion, thus far, has only suggested that relationships exist between patient attitudes, acquisition of hospital information, and length of hospitalization. Stated more specifically in the form of hypotheses, we expect the following:

1. Patients selectively acquire information about the hospital.

2. Significant relationships exist between the kind of hospital information patients acquire and their attitudes toward mental illness, the mental hospital, and hospitalization.

3. Significant relationships exist between the kind of hospital information patients acquire and how long they have lived in the hospital as well as how long they will remain in the hospital.

METHOD

The Hospital Information Test (described later) was group administered to 206 randomly selected mental patients. In addition, the male patients were given, in groups, the Opinions about Mental Illness scale (see later).[16] The patients who had not been discharged one year after the initial testing were again given the Hospital Information Test. This enabled us to examine any

---

[16]The cost in terms of patient time to complete the 100-item test, and in some cases the discomfort it produced, was such that the decision was made to omit the Opinions about Mental Illness scale for the female sample.

changes that might have occurred over time as well as an opportunity to determine the relationship, if any, between patterns of acquired hospital information and length of stay in the hospital.

Because this is a correlational study, a few words about the variables under scrutiny are in order.

MEASURES

The Hospital Information Test (HIT)[17]   A 24-item test was constructed in order to measure two very general areas of patient knowledge about the hospital. Thirteen items assessed patient information about important *hospital staff* members attached to the patients' building (that is, the names of staff members and the location of their offices), while nine items were concerned with *residential aspects of hospital life* (for example, names and locations of buildings). Two items concerning visiting hours and visiting days were also included.

The criteria for item selection were (1) the answers had to be potentially obvious, that is, patients would not have to acquire exotic information about the hospital in order to answer them; (2) the information required could be learned readily without the patient having to make any personal contact with the staff; and (3) the items would make minimal intellectual demands on the patients (in this way we hoped to insure that HIT scores would not vary as a function of intelligence).

Opinions about Mental Illness Scale (OMI)   In order to assess patients' attitudes toward mental illness, the mental hospital, and patienthood, the 100-item OMI, developed by Struening and Cohen (1962), was employed. These items were constructed so that they can be meaningfully answered by both hospitalized and nonhospitalized populations.

Demographic Measures   Information concerning the patient's age, education, length of hospitalization, number of hospitalizations, diagnostic categories, and marital status were obtained for all subjects. Phillips' premorbid adjustment scores (1953), based on the prehospital social and sexual life of the patient were computed from case histories for a randomly selected portion of the sample. The Phillips' scale was included because it is a widely employed variable in mental illness research.

[17]A copy of this test may be found in Appendix A.

SUBJECTS   All subjects (93 men and 113 women) were hospitalized open-ward patients. The mean age was 40.4 years with a standard deviation of 13.8. The mean educational level was 10.6 years, the standard deviation being 4.5. The median length of hospitalization for males was 4.1 years and for females 3.8 years. The diagnostic category breakdown was 72 percent schizophrenic, 22 percent psychotic but not schizophrenic, and 6 percent nonpsychotic. There were no significant sex differences with respect to these demographic variables. The mean of the Phillips' premorbid adjustment scores for a random sample of 40 male patients was 15.37 with a standard deviation of 7.30; and for a random sample of 40 female patients, 11.43 with a standard deviation of 6.98. The differences between the two groups was significant ($t = 2.47, p < .02$).

RESULTS

Hypothesis 1: Mental patients selectively acquire information about the mental hospital.

In order to test our prediction, a factor analysis was first computed for the HIT. The responses of the total sample ($N = 206$) to the 24 HIT items, four demographic variables (length of hospitalization, number of hospitalizations, age, and education), and a series of random numbers were correlated in a 29-by-29 product-moment matrix. Principal component factors were extracted with unity as the diagonal value. The factors judged salient were then rotated to orthogonal structure by the verimax procedure.

The results of the factor analysis are presented in Table 5. Two factors clearly emerged: Factor I was identified primarily by information pertaining to places in the hospital (Residential factor), while Factor II was relevant to knowledge about the names and offices of the hospital staff (Hospital Staff factor). Moreover, it was reassuring to note that education, a gross index of intelligence, played an insignificant role in the loadings of Factors I and II. Let us examine now if and how patients vary on these factors.

Because most of the items had a high loading on one factor and a low-to-zero loading on the other, two subscales of the HIT

TABLE 5

Orthogonally Rotated Factor Matrices of
the HIT Items
(N = 206)

ITEM	FACTOR I	FACTOR II
1. Name of psychiatrist	.06	.55*
2. Location of psychiatrist's office	.11	.54*
3. Name of nurse in unit	.32	.49
4. Name of doctor in charge of unit	.12	.36
5. Location of doctor in charge's office	.20	.49
6. Name of nursing supervisor	.23	.58*
7. Location of nursing supervisor's office	.18	.43*
8. Name of psychologist in unit	.05	.35
9. Location of psychologist's office	.14	.52*
10. Name of the social worker in unit	.24	.74*
11. Location of the social worker's office	.22	.70*
12. Name of superintendent	.68*	.02
13. Location of the superintendent's office	.63*	.14
14. Number of floors in the unit	.19	.44*
15. Name of the chapel	.75*	.00
16. Name of the O.T. building	.73*	.09
17. Name of the administration building	.70*	.21*
18. Name of the movie theatre building	.56*	.01
19. Name of the canteen building	.72*	.01
20. Knowledge of visiting days	.44*	.19
21. Knowledge of visiting hours	.46*	.41*
22. Knowledge of number of patients in building	.54*	.12
23. Knowledge of number of patients in hospital	.51*	.07
24. Knowledge of quitting time of day-shift of nurses and aides	.55*	.05
Demographic Variables		
25. Age	.14	−.71
26. Education	.13	.16
27. Number of prior hospitalizations	.00	−.10
28. Length of present hospitalization	.33	−.65
29. Random numbers	−.01	.06

*Items chosen for factor scale.

were extrapolated readily by factor scoring each of the items.[18]
The asterisked items in Table 5 represent the ones selected for

[18]Two items were, however, included as common items to both subscales: one because it loaded highly on Factors I and II and the other because it appeared to be logically related to both factors.

each scale. The test-retest coefficients for the factors one year after initial testing ($N = 96$) were .86 for the Residential factor and .70 for the Hospital Staff factor. The internal consistency coefficients (Spearman-Brown Covariance Approximation Form, Tyron, 1957) for the Residential Factor was .88 and for the Hospital Staff factor, .84.

To return to our hypothesis, if patients are selective in the kinds of information they acquire, a low correlation should be found between their Residential and Hospital Staff factor scores. Although the correlation[19] was statistically significant ($p < .01$), it is clear that it did not account for very much of the variance ($r = .35$); that is, the majority of the variance can not be attributed to a kind of g factor. Patients can and frequently do score high on one factor and low on the other; they do, therefore, selectively acquire information about the hospital.

The overall percentage of correct responses to the HIT items (see Table 19, Chapter 3) provided data about the kinds of hospital information patients typically acquire. Because later in this chapter these data will be presented and discussed at length, only some of the results will be summarized here. In short, significantly more patients were familiar with the locations of the bowling alley (82 percent), gym (80 percent), swimming pool (80 percent), patient dances (70 percent), movie theater (70 percent) and canteen (68 percent) than with the name of their own psychiatrist (48 percent), the psychologist in their building (26 percent), the locations of the occupational therapy building (46 percent), and the social worker's office (22 percent). Clearly, our notion concerning patients' hedonistic hospital orientation is confirmed by these data. Patients, in general, selectively acquire more information about the recreational and hedonic aspects of the hospital than about the formal therapeutic aspects.

Another way to examine patient variance in the kind of information they acquire is to focus on subgroup differences; for example, subgroups based on sex, time spent in the hospital, and so on. With respect to sex, several analyses were conducted. Although a factor analysis by sex, using the same procedure described above, yielded almost identical factors, there were significant differences between males and females on the factor

[19]The correlation was corrected for the two-item overlap on the subscales (see footnote 18).

TABLE 6

*Percentage of Correct Responses
to HIT Items by Sex*

ITEMS	PERCENT CORRECT	
	MALE ($N = 93$)	FEMALE ($N = 113$)
1. Name of subject's psychiatrist	47	62*
2. Location of psychiatrist's office (floor)	41	38
3. Name of a nurse in subject's unit	34	9†
4. Name of the doctor in charge of unit	29	58†
5. Location of doctor in charge's office	43	52
6. Name of the nursing supervisor	58	59
7. Location of nursing supervisor's office	60	59
8. Name of the psychologist in the unit	2	23†
9. Location of psychologist's office	14	21
10. Name of the social worker in unit	19	43†
11. Location of social worker's office	29	43*
12. Name of the superintendent of the hospital	41	36
13. The building the superintendent's office is located in	34	33
14. The number of floors in patient's unit	66	56
15. The name of the chapel	45	32*
16. Name of the OT building	46	32*
17. Name of the administration building	51	34*
18. Name of the movie theatre building	80	74
19. Name of the building the canteen is in	72	59*
20. Knowledge of visiting day	57	66
21. Knowledge of visiting hours	30	30
22. The number of patients in the unit	48	43
23. The number of patients in the hospital	39	32
24. The hour the day shift of nurses and aides leave	52	57

*$p < .05$
†$p < .01$

scores. Male patients scored significantly higher on Residential information ($\overline{X} = 50.09$ percent correct responses) than on Hospital Staff information ($\overline{X} = 32.37$; $p < .01$). Female patients, however, showed no significant differences between Residential examination of Table 6 indicates that of the six items pertaining ($\overline{X} = 47.90$) and Hospital Staff ($\overline{X} = 49.73$) information. An to staff members on which men and women differed significantly, women were better informed on five of these, whereas the men were superior to women with respect to the four significant items dealing with places in the hospital.

Bearing in mind what we know about sex differences in normal persons, these results certainly are not unusual. That is, women typically have more information about the members of their community than the men, who, in turn, generally focus upon the more recreational aspects of their community.

A more complex comparison of information scores by sex and length of hospitalization presented in Table 7 also yielded significant and intriguing results. Specifically, female patients hospitalized for a period of one year or less scored significantly higher on Hospital staff information than on Residential information ($z =$ 2.45, $p < .02$), while the reverse was true for females hospitalized for more than one year. In addition, correlations between length of hospitalization and factor scores showed that, at least cross-sectionally, female patients acquire more Residential information as they spend more time in the hospital ($r = .38$, $p < .01$) while,

TABLE 7

*Means and Standard Deviations of HIT
Factor Scores by Sex and Length of
Present Hospitalization*

LENGTH OF HOSPITALIZATION		MALE		FEMALE	
		FACTOR I*	FACTOR II†	FACTOR I	FACTOR II
1 year or less	$\overline{X}$	5.83	3.77	4.61	6.00
	SD	3.14	2.36	3.73	2.97
		(N = 31)		(N = 29)	
2 through 7.9 years	$\overline{X}$	7.15	3.31	5.10	4.10
	SD	3.59	2.53	3.50	3.45
		(N = 38)		(N = 42)	
8 years or more	$\overline{X}$	5.91	1.83	6.24	3.86
	SD	3.76	1.85	3.92	3.20
		(N = 24)		(N = 42)	

*Residential information
†Hospital Staff information
Source: Braginsky, Holzberg, Finison, and Ring (1967).

at the same time, they decrease in Hospital Staff information ($r = -.41$, $p < .01$). There is no significant increase in Residential information over time for male patients ($r = .10$), although they do show a significant decrease in Hospital Staff information ($r = -.37$, $p < .01$). It should be noted, however, that female subjects at almost any point in their hospitalization score significantly higher on Hospital Staff information than their male counterparts (see Table 7).[20]

In summary, it is evident that patients do differ with respect to the amounts and kinds of information they acquire about the hospital. Moreover, portions of this variance have been identified with the sex of the patient, length of hospitalization, and the interaction between sex and length of hospitalization.

Hypothesis 2: Significant relationships exist between the kinds of information patients acquire and their attitudes about mental illness, the mental hospital, and patienthood.[21]

Correlations were computed between the OMI items and the HIT factors. Because there were 100 items and we could, therefore, expect ten significant correlations at the .05 level by chance, an alpha level of .01 was used to define a stringent standard of significance. The results, which may be seen in Table 8, showed that ten attitude items were significantly correlated with Residential information, and 12 different items with Hospital Staff information scores. Without examining the content of the clusters, it is possible to conclude that, at least structurally, differential relationships exist between patient attitudes and acquired information. That is, patients who differed with respect to the kind of information they acquired about the hospital also differed in their attitudes about the hospital, mental illness, and patienthood.

Although certain within-cluster consistencies and between-cluster differences appear when we turn to the content of the items, a similar theme emerges that cuts across both factors; namely,

---

[20]Female Ss score significantly higher on Hospital Staff information than men in the one-year-or-less group ($t = 3.37$, $p < .01$) and in the eight-years-or-more group ($t = 3.32$, $p < .01$).

[21]No specific predictions were made concerning the relationships, because this phase of our research was primarily exploratory.

that mental patients believe that, despite their illness, they are just like ordinary people; that they too are human beings, a point that we have been stressing throughout this book.

The Residential cluster of items, in addition, seem to reflect concern about the causality or, perhaps, the responsibility for one's illness. More specifically, high Residential scorers agreed with items that externalize the locus of causality, emphasizing that the reason some people become mentally ill is because they

TABLE 8

Attitude Items that Correlate Significantly
with the Two Hospital Information Test
Factors (N = 83)

ATTITUDE ITEMS THAT CORRELATE WITH RESIDENTIAL KNOWLEDGE OF THE HOSPITAL (FACTOR I)	r
1. The patients in mental hospitals should have something to say about the way the hospital is run.	.39
2. People who were once patients in mental hospitals are no more dangerous than the average citizen.	.37
3. The mental illness of many people is caused by the separation or divorce of their parents during childhood.	.34
4. Most mental patients are willing to work.	.32
5. It is possible to become mentally ill by believing very strongly that you are likely to suffer eternal punishment and torture after death.	.31
6. If the children of mentally ill patients were raised by normal parents they would probably not become mentally ill.	.31
7. Many mental patients are capable of skilled labor, even though in some ways they are very disturbed.	.28
8. Even if a person who has been a patient in a mental hospital seems fully recovered, he should not be given a driver's license.	—.30
9. Success is more dependent on luck than real ability.	—.29
10. There is little use in writing to public officials because they are not really interested in the problems of the average man.	—.28

TABLE 8 (continued)

ATTITUDE ITEMS WHICH CORRELATE WITH KNOWLEDGE
OF HOSPITAL STAFF (FACTOR II)   *r*

1. Many people in our society are lonely and unrelated to their fellow human beings.	.35
2. Everyone should have someone in his life whose happiness means as much to him as his own.	.33
3. Even though patients in mental hospitals behave in funny ways, it is wrong to laugh about them.	.28
4. People who have been patients in mental hospitals should be advised not to have children.	—.39
5. The law should allow a women to divorce her husband as soon as he has been confined in a mental hospital with a severe mental illness.	—.37
6. People with mental illness should never be treated in the same hospital as people with physical illness.	—.36
7. Every mental hospital should be surrounded by a high fence and guards.	—.35
8. A person who has been a patient in a mental hospital should not be allowed by law to hold high political office.	—.31
9. Anyone who is in a hospital for mental illness should not be allowed to vote.	—.29
10. A woman would be foolish to marry a man who has had a severe mental illness, even though he seems fully recovered.	—.29
11. When a patient in a mental hospital does exactly what he is told, it is a good sign that his mental health is improving.	—.29
12. The main purpose of a mental hospital should be to protect the public from a mentally ill person.	—.28

happened to have come from a pathogenic environment (for example, "The mental illness of many people is caused by the separation or divorce of their parents during childhood").

The attitudes related to Hospital Staff information scores, on the other hand, focus on the social implications of being or having been a mental patient. In addition to their strong opposition to the social restriction of mental patients and the loss of their civil rights, high Hospital Staff scorers expressed the need for humanism and relatedness between people. Thus, although the two groups share the belief that mental patients are like other human beings, the high Hospital Staff scorers take an aggressive stance, demanding that the dignity and rights of mental patients be respected, while the high Residential scorers remind others that, but for the grace of a good childhood, and so on, they, too, could have become mental patients.

Hypothesis 3: Significant relationships exist between the kind of hospital information acquired by patients and how long they have been or will remain in the hospital.

Some cross-sectional evidence is available in support of our hypothesis. For example, the loadings of length of hospitalization were high on the Residential (.33) and Hospital Staff (−.65) factors, with a particularly high loading on the latter factor; length of hospitalization was positively related to high Residential information scores and low Hospital Staff information scores.

Our longitudinal data also supports this prediction. Information about the status of the patients tested on the HIT was obtained after one year, during which time 91 patients had been discharged (leavers) while 106 remained (stayers). In order to examine the relationship between acquired information and discharge while controlling for length of hospitalization, we divided our sample into two groups; one group consisted of patients who had been in the hospital for three years or less (with 32 stayers and 65 leavers), and the other group had been hospitalized for four years or more (with 74 stayers and 26 leavers).[22] The mean length of hospitalization for both stayers and leavers in each of the two groups was approximately the same.

Furthermore, we developed an index of patient information acquisition that was not dependent upon the absolute acquisition of information; this index was expressed by the following ratio score:

$$\frac{\text{Residential score} - \text{Hospital Staff score}}{\text{Residential score} + \text{Hospital Staff score}} + 1.00$$

Ratios above 1.00[23] indicated a superiority of Residential information to Hospital Staff information, whereas ratios below 1.00

[22]The cut-off point was chosen in an attempt to equalize the number of Ss in each of the two groups and leave enough Ss in each of the subgroups to do meaningful statistical analyses.

showed a superiority of Hospital Staff information to Residential information. The mean ratio score for each of the groups is presented in Table 9. Point biserial correlations were then computed between ratio scores and whether a patient remained or was discharged during the year. The overall correlation for the three-year-or-less group was $-.38$ ($p < .01$), while for the four-year-or-more group it was $-.15$ (n.s.). Upon closer examination, however, we find that the significant correlation for the 3 year or less group is primarily a function of the female patients ($r = -.58$, $p < .01$). The correlation for males in this group was only $-.21$ (n.s.). There were no significant intragroup correlations for the four-year-or-more group, nor were there any differences between the males and females. The greater homogeneity of information profiles for the long-term patients (see page 87) seems to preclude the emergence of any significant relationship here.

We can state, then, that there appears to be some predictive relationship between staying or leaving the hospital and information scores, although, admittedly, it is primarily of value for

TABLE 9

Mean Ratio* of HIT Factor Scores of Patients Who Either Left or Remained in the Hospital One Year after Initial Testing

STATUS	LENGTH OF HOSPITALIZATION AT TIME OF INITIAL TESTING			
	1 TO 3 YEARS		4 YEARS OR MORE	
	Male	Female	Male	Female
Discharged	.93 ($N = 31$)	.57 ($N = 34$)	1.32 ($N = 12$)	1.00 ($N = 14$)
Remained	1.01 ($N = 15$)	1.01 ($N = 17$)	1.27 ($N = 35$)	1.11 ($N = 39$)

*Ratios above 1.00 show superiority of Residential information to Hospital Staff information; ratios below 1.00 represent superiority of Hospital Staff information to Residential information.

[23]Because the factor scales had an unequal number of items, .20 was subtracted from the ratio, yielding a mid-point of 1.00.

female patients who have not been hospitalized for more than three years.

The obvious question now is whether the more consistent profile scores (Residential superior to Hospital Staff information) found in the four-year-or-more group is a function of patient selectivity or of hospital effects. That is, do the patients who remain tend to be those who simply learn, more or less on their own initiative, about the residential aspects of hospital life; or does the hospital systematically avoid or ignore Old-timers? Let us examine first the hospital avoidance alternative. It is clear from observation alone that, if patients are avoided, they may still initiate interaction with the staff if they so desire; that is, they can readily ask the nurses, aides, and even patients the names of staff members. Moreover, ward rounds are made once a week, so that any patient who makes himself available can learn the name of the doctor and other staff members at this time.

We can offer also an empirical rebuff to the hospital effects alternative by using longitudinal data, the HIT test-retest scores. The analyses of these data (both tests of means and correlations) showed that patients who remained in the hospital for a year did not change significantly in their information scores. If we can assume that one year is sufficient time to examine the possible effect of the hospital (that is, the staff avoidance of certain patients) on information acquisition, we can conclude that any such hospital effects are, at most, minimal.

In summary, then, there is evidence that a relationship exists between the length of time patients have been in the hospital and what they have learned about the hospital. Second, it appears that for particular subgroups of patients there are predictive relationships independent of length of hospitalization between what patients have learned and whether they remain in the hospital. Third, the results suggest that our cross-sectional findings (that is, the relationship between length of hospitalization and information factor scores) are a function of patient selectivity rather than accumulated hospital effects.

DISCUSSION

The complexities of the relationships between hospital information, sex, attitudes, time in residence, and discharge can be parsimoniously and, we feel, plausibly understood in terms of patient needs, interests, and consequent self-initiated styles of adaptation. It seems reasonable to assume that, if a patient has learned little about the hospital staff, this information is not important to him. Certainly, we would make this assumption if we were asked to explain why a nonhospitalized person has failed to learn the name of his postman or the name of a doctor on his street. Thus we do not find it necessary, or even warranted, to try to invoke complex interpretations that assume pathological processes or environmental neglect of patients in order to understand their behavior. It is, admittedly, difficult to believe that a patient's lack of information about the hospital staff reflects a lack of concern; but, perhaps, it is only because *we* feel that the hospital staff is so vital to the patient. There is no reason, however, why we should feel compelled to assume that all patients share our valuations.

It is clear that patients who wish to remain in the hospital or who want to establish a comfortable, hedonic life style, may adapt in a manner that simply does not allow for frequent contact with the hospital staff. That is, they may actively avoid hospital therapeutic programs, for example, and may instead participate in the hedonic activities of the hospital (for example, socializing in the canteen, dances, movies). Consequently, these patients will acquire minimal amounts of knowledge about the staff while at the same time learning more about the residential aspects of the hospital (for example, canteen building, movie theater). Other patients who wish to be "cured" or, at least, serviced by the hospital will adapt in a way that allows for intensive and extensive contact with the hospital staff. They would, therefore, learn more about the staff than the hedonically or residentially oriented patients.

It should be made clear at this point that we are not implying that the hospital plays no role in patients' acquisition of information. The point we are stressing, however, is that adaptation and acquisition of information are functions of the interaction between the patient and the hospital. Although uninterested patients may not acquire information about the hospital staff, the staff itself may indirectly facilitate this lack of acquisition. We assume, therefore, that if the staff interacted frequently with all of the patients, then, regardless of their styles of adaptation, the patients would be more likely to learn the names of the staff. In this case at least, the hospital may have an effect, but it is of an omissive rather than commissive nature.

There is, however, one major flaw in this study, and that is that patient styles of adaptation have not been measured directly; our correlations therefore, may be subject to numerous interpretations. Let us examine one such alternative explanation based upon the psychiatric paradigm presented in Chapter 1; namely, patient behavior is determined primarily by pathological processes and/or institutional demands.

If we assume that patient attitudes, the nature of hospital intervention, and the length of hospitalization are basically a function of the degree of the patient's psychopathology, predictions identical to those we made could be generated. For example, employing these assumptions, we could predict that poor prognosis patients (severely and chronically ill) will tend to be less involved with the hospital staff because staff time will be spent with the more "curable" mental patients (acute and less severely ill). If this is so, we would expect the poor prognosis patients to acquire less information about the hospital staff than the good prognosis patients. In addition, because the less disturbed patients will be spending much of their time with the staff, they will have less time available to explore the residential aspects of the hospital. As a result, this group will have little residential information and a great deal of hospital staff information.

An explanation of the relationship between information scores and discharge could also be offered using the same rationale. Simply stated, "sicker" patients remain in the hospital longer than less severely ill ones; "sicker" patients also have less contact with staff than the other patients and, therefore, they acquire less information about the hospital staff. Thus, a relationship would be anticipated between acquired hospital information and the length of hospitalization or discharge. In much the same manner, similar explanations might be given for our other findings.

In order to examine the relevance of the "psychopathology hypothesis," two further analyses were conducted. First, an attempt was made to relate diagnostic categories to information scores, attitude items, length of hospitalization, and discharge. Using a three-category breakdown (schizophrenic, psychotic but not schizophrenic, and nonpsychotic), no significant relationships were found. This, however, is not surprising because the majority of patients (72 percent) were diagnosed as schizophrenic, restricting, of course, any relationship between diagnostic categories and other psychological variables.

In the second analysis, the severity or chronicity of mental illness (Phillips, 1953) was related to the same variables. A randomly selected group of 80 patients (40 males and 40 females) were assigned Phillips scores of premorbid adjustment on the basis of their case histories. The overall correlations indicated that once again significant relationships do not exist between Phillips premorbidity scores and information acquired, attitude items, length of hospitalization, and staying or leaving the hospital. Despite the significant sex difference on Phillips scores (men had significantly poorer premorbid adjustment than women), within sex correlations also proved to be insignificant. On the basis of, at least, these two commonly used indices patient psychopathology appears to be irrelevant to the phenomena under investigation.

Although the results of this preliminary study were encouraging, the confirmation of the predicted relationships provided only indirect evidence for the acceptance of our model; however, to the extent that we have demonstrated the untenability of the psychopathological and institutional demands hypotheses, we feel that we may have increased confidence both in the appropriateness of our model and in the plausibility of our assumptions about the nature of the mental patient. Nevertheless, we must own up to the deficiency of this study, namely, that we have examined only the assumed antecedents and consequences of patients' adaptation styles. In the next study, therefore, we focused directly on the presumed mediating variable, patient styles of adaptation to the mental hospital.

PATIENT STYLES OF ADAPTATION
TO A MENTAL HOSPITAL

In this somewhat more definitive study, conducted by B. Braginsky, J. Holzberg, D. Ridley, and D. Braginsky (1968), the following hypotheses were tested:

1. Mental patients differ in their styles of adaptation to the hospital.

2. Styles of adaptation are significantly related to the kinds

of information patients acquire about the mental hospital.

3. Styles of adaptation are significantly related to patient attitudes about mental illness, the mental hospital, and patienthood.

4. Styles of adaptation are significantly related to length of hospitalization.

5. Styles of adaptation are not related to indices of the patients' psychopathological status or to putative differential hospital demands.

6. Styles of adaptation are significantly related to the patients' therapeutic involvement in the hospital.

These predictions cover all aspects of the model presented earlier; that is, we have interconnected the antecedent, mediating, and consequent variables by means of related predictions.

METHOD

The procedure here involved individual administration of both questionnaire surveys and interviews, which are described below, to 100 randomly selected mental patients (50 men and 50 women).

MEASURES

Hospital Information Test II (HIT II) An information test similar to, but more extensive than, the one used in the previous study was constructed. The HIT II contained the original 24 items in addition to 48 new ones, most of which were chosen on the basis of the information factors extracted earlier (Residential and Hospital Staff). The areas of information measured on the HIT II were:

1. *Residential information.* Forty items about the names and locations of places that offer a variety of services usually found in any large community (for example, chapel, canteen, and shoe repair shop).

2. *Hospital staff information.* Twenty items about the names and location of hospital staff whose primary function is patient treatment and management (for example, the name of the patient's psychiatrist and location of his office).

3. *Administration staff information.* Seven items dealing with patient knowledge about the administrators of the hospital (for example, names and locations of department heads).

4. *Miscellaneous information.* Five items that did not fall clearly into any of the above domains but that we felt were important in understanding patient information profiles (for example, knowledge of his own diagnosis).

Patient Attitude Test (PAT)[24]   The PAT was an 86-item attitude test on which each item was rated on a six-point Likert scale. Fifty-six items ascertained whether patients had attitudes that would predispose them to use the hospital to satisfy needs and goals irrelevant to the formal purposes of hospitalization (that is, to live in the hospital as if it were a resort or non-hospital community). Thirty items were taken from the OMI (Struening and Cohen, 1962) that focused on patient attitudes toward their similarity to people in general and their need for human relatedness.

Interview Schedule   A structured interview schedule was designed to obtain information about:

1. *Patient styles of adaptation.* Patients were asked to give a detailed (hourly) account of where and how they spent their waking time during a "typical" 24-hour day in the hospital. Each patient was then assigned three scores based on the number of hours spent (1) on the ward, (2) at work, and (3) off the ward in informal social activities. These categories accounted for almost all of the patients' responses. In order to insure the accuracy and stability of their responses, a sample of 20 percent were observed (a time sampling procedure) and 15 percent were reinterviewed three months later.[25]

2. *Perceived hospital demands.* Patients were asked, "Where *must* you spend time in the hospital—where does the hospital order you to go?" "What activities are you *ordered* to engage in?" "How much time must you spend there?" These questions permitted us to examine the patient's perception of the hospital's demands. In addition, we could determine also whether differential hospital pressures are associated with different styles of adaptation.

3. *Psychological ecology of the hospital.* The following ques-

---

[24] A copy of the PAT may be found in Appendix A.
[25] The temporal reliability coefficients for ward, work, and off-ward socializing were, respectively, .89, .85, and .82. The time sampling procedure (three times a day for one week) indicated that patients were very accurate in their self-reports.

tions were asked: "Name the areas of the hospital where a patient can spend time." "What can he do in those areas?" "What do patients do in those areas?" These questions enabled us to examine the perceived number and kinds of pathways for adaptation as well as the "richness" of the hospital milieu; that is, we obtained patients' cognitive maps of the hospital.

4. *Patient motility.* We were interested in the degree to which patients perceive their movements as restricted by the hospital. "Where *can't* you spend time in the hospital?" "What areas of the hospital are off-limits to patients—why?" The number and kind of locations mentioned were indexes of the intensity and extent of patient restriction.

5. *Therapeutic involvement.* Patients were asked about the number and kinds of therapy programs in which they were or had been members, the time spent in these programs, and whether participation was on a voluntary or assigned basis.

Demographic Measures Information about age, education, length of hospitalization, number of hospitalizations, diagnostic categories, and marital status were obtained for all subjects.

SUBJECTS All 50 men and 50 women were hospitalized open-ward patients. Their mean age was 42.5 years with a standard deviation of 4.0. The mean education level was 9.2 years, and the standard deviation was 3.6. The median length of hospitalization was 5.4 years. The general diagnostic categories of the group were 78 percent schizophrenic, 12 percent psychotic but not schizophrenic, and 10 percent nonpsychotic. There were no significant differences between men and women on these demographic variables.

RESULTS

Hypothesis 1: Patients differ in their styles of adaptation to the mental hospital.

The hourly accounts of the "typical" mental patient's day indicated that patients differ markedly with respect to where they spend their time. For example, time spent on the ward ranged from 1.5 to 14 hours daily; time spent at work, from 0 to 8 hours; and time spent in recreational areas off the wards, from 0 to 11 hours.

Our index of adaptation styles for individual subjects was based on a comparison of each patient's time with the total sample median time for each of the three categories. The results were that 21 percent of the patients were above the median for time spent on the ward and were below the median on time spent both at work and off the ward socializing; 19 percent of the patients were above the median on time spent at work and below it on time spent both on the ward and off the ward socializing; and 25 percent were above the median on time spent off the ward socializing and below it on time spent on the ward and at work. Thus the majority of this sample (65 percent) manifested what we consider "pure" styles of adaptation; the "warders," the "workers,'" and the "mobile socializers."

The remaining patients (35 percent) exhibited variants of these types. Seventeen percent were above the median on both ward and off-ward socializing time; 10 percent were above the medians for work and off-ward socializing; and 8 percent were above the median on ward and work time.

The data clearly support our hypothesis. Patients not only showed individual differences but also manifested identifiable styles of adaptation to the hospital.

Hypothesis 2: Styles of adaptation are significantly related to the kinds of information patients acquire about the hospital.

The correlations between information scores and adaptation styles allowed us to examine whether information acquisition was differentially associated with time spent on the ward, at work, and in off-ward socializing. The information items that were significantly correlated (alpha level of .01) with ward, work, and off-ward time are presented in Tables 10, 11, and 12, respectively.

Clearly, as time spent on the ward increased, information acquisition decreased (all correlations are negative). That is, a great deal of time spent on the ward is associated with a general impoverishment of information about the hospital; these patients knew little about the hospital staff and the residential aspects of the hospital.

TABLE 10

Information Items that Correlated Significantly (p < .01)
with Time Spent on the Ward (N = 100)

	r
1. Location of the school	—.41
2. Names of the buildings employees live in	—.41
3. Location of the nurse's office	—.39
4. Name of a nurse in other units	—.37
5. Location of patient dances	—.37
6. Location of the superintendent's office	—.36
7. Number of floors in subject's buildings	—.36
8. Location of the gift shop	—.34
9. Name of the doctor in charge of subject's unit	—.32
10. Location of the business manager's office	—.31
11. Location of the laboratory	—.31
12. Location of the Swank Shop (used clothing store)	—.29
13. Name of the psychologist in subject's unit	—.29
14. Name of the business manager	—.29
15. Name of the head of OT department	—.29
16. Location of the hospital pharmacy	—.29
17. Name of the nursing supervisor in subject's building	—.28
18. Name of the nurse in subject's building	—.28
19. Name of a nursing supervisor in other units	—.26
20. Location of the psychologist's office in subject's unit	—.26
21. Name of the superintendent	—.26
22. Location of the printing shop	—.26
23. Location of the tailor shop	—.25

Source: Braginsky, Holzberg, Ridley, and Braginsky (1968).

Work time, however, was generally positively related to information acquisition and, specifically, to residential information. In addition, it was positively related to knowledge about the staff who were located in buildings other than the patients' and neg-

TABLE 11

Information Items that Correlated Significantly ($p < .01$) with Time Spent at Work ($N = 100$)

	r
1. Location of the tailor shop	.49
2. Location of the hospital pharmacy	.43
3. Names of the buildings employees live in	.43
4. Location of the hospital switchboard	.34
5. Knowledge of library hours	.32
6. Location of the business manager's office	.32
7. Name of a nurse in other buildings	.31
8. Name of the doctor in charge of other units	.29
9. Location of patient dances	.29
10. Location of the Swank Shop (used clothing store)	.29
11. Location of the shoe repair shop	.27
12. Location of the school	.27
13. Location of the hospital post office	.26
14. Location of the canteen	.26
15. Name of the nursing supervisor in other units	.26
16. Name of the business manager	.25
17. Location of the bowling alley	.25
18. Name of subject's psychiatrist	−.31
19. Location of subject's psychiatrist	−.29
20. Location of the psychology department	−.25

Source: Braginsky, Holzberg, Ridley, and Braginsky (1968).

TABLE 12

Information Items that Correlated Significantly (p < .01)
with Time Spent Socializing off the Ward (N = 100)

	r
1. Name of the subject's psychiatrist	.32
2. Knowledge of medication received	.31
3. Location of the out-patient clinic	.31
4. Location of the psychologist's office in subject's unit	.30
5. Number of floors in subject's unit	.30
6. Name of the head of nursing	.29
7. Number of therapy programs for patients	.28
8. Location of the doctor-in-charge's office in subject's unit	.26
9. Name of a nurse in subject's unit	.26
10. Location of office of subject's psychiatrist	.25
11. Location of social worker's office in subject's unit	.25

Source: Braginsky, Holzberg, Ridley, and Braginsky (1968).

atively related to knowledge about their own doctor and where he was located.

Off-ward socializing was associated positively with information concerning the hospital staff located in the patients' own buildings. Moreover, it was related to knowledge of medication received, therapeutic programs offered by the hospital, and interestingly, the location of the out-patient clinic.

A more detailed analysis of the association between adaptation styles and information acquisition, using the data of the 65 patients who manifested "pure" styles, was conducted. In order to make comparisons with the prior study, we used the same information items as well as the same ratio score (see p. 91) in our analyses.[26]

---

[26]Ratios above 1.00 indicate a superiority of Residential information to Hospital Staff information; ratios of .99 or less indicate a superiority of Hospital Staff information to Residential information.

The mean ratio for "warders" ($N = 21$) was 1.30; for "workers" ($N = 19$), 1.47; and for "mobile socializers" ($N = 25$), .93. The analysis of variance of these data yielded an F of 12.88 ($p < .001$). The difference between the "warders" and "workers" was not significant, although each of these groups was significantly different from the "mobile socializers" ($p < .01$). Thus, warders and workers selectively acquire more information about the residential aspects of the hospital than about the hospital staff, while the reverse is true for mobile socializers.

The next analysis involved factor scoring the information items (according to the factors extracted in our earlier study[27]) and intercorrelating them with time spent in the three areas. Time spent on the ward was related negatively to the Residential information factor ($r = -.38$, $p < .01$), to the Hospital Staff factor ($r = -.29$, $p < .01$), and, obviously, to total information scores ($r = -.30$, $p < .01$). Work time was positively related to Residential information ($r = .36$, $p < .01$), unrelated to Hospital Staff information ($r = .07$), and positively related to total information ($r = .22$, $p < .01$).

The findings, then, support our hypothesis; the manner in which patients adapt to the hospital is significantly related to the kinds and amounts of information they acquire.

Hypothesis 3: Styles of adaptation are significantly related to patient attitudes concerning the mental hospital, mental illness, and patienthood.

The attitude items that are correlated significantly (alpha = .01) with ward, work, and off-ward socializing are presented in Table 13. The attitude clusters associated with each style of adaptation represent distinctly different profiles of the mental patient's beliefs. For instance, as time spent on the ward increased, patients increased in the maintenance of attitudes that stressed (1) their difference from "normal" people, (2) the immutability of their psychological condition as well as the immutability of their role as patients, (3) the need for social restrictiveness, (4) the beliefs that patients should not enjoy themselves but rather should

---

[27]These factors have been cross-validated in a recent factor analysis of our new data.

expect to suffer if they ever wished to get well again, and (5) the desire to be left alone by both staff and patients.

Work time was associated with attitudes that (1) patients are different from nonhospitalized people,[28] (2) the hospital should have a "hands-off" policy toward the patients, (3) patients should have greater control over the "gates" in the hospital (that is, entry to and exit from the institution), (4) the hospital should make sure that patients are comfortable, and (5) while in the hospital, one should not accept the role of patienthood.

The attitudes that clustered around off-ward socializing, on the other hand, stressed (1) the similarity of patients to "normal" people, (2) opposition to the social restriction of mental patients and their loss of civil liberties, (3) the need for human relatedness, (4) the temporary nature of the patient role, (5) the patient's need for enjoyment and comfort while in the hospital, and (6) the value of interpersonal forms of therapy as much as chemotherapy.

One can note from Table 13 that ward and off-ward socializing appear to be bipolar styles of adaptation. That is, both of these styles are associated with the same attitudes, but in opposite directions. Work time, however, is associated with items that are, for the most part, unrelated to the two other modes of adaptation.

In summary, then, patient attitudes concerning the hospital, mental illness, and patienthood are significantly related to the manner in which they adapt to the hospital; our hypothesis, therefore, stands confirmed.

---

[28]At first glance the attitude that mental patients are different from normal people, endorsed by both the warders and workers, appears to contradict our earlier finding (see p. 91) that patients feel they are just like ordinary people. This later finding, however, reflects only the relative difference between the self-perceptions of warders, workers, and mobile socializers, rather than an absolute statement of their self-perceptions. Nevertheless, we feel that an attempt should be made to explain why the warders and workers disagree less than the mobile socializers with items dealing with their differences from "normals." Because warders and workers represent patients who have been hospitalized for long periods and who have very low discharge rates, their questionnaire behavior may be interpreted as (1) a form of impression management designed to assure their stay in the hospital (see Chapter 2); (2) a kind of brain-washing, resulting from prolonged contact with the psychiatric paradigm; or (3) a manifestation of their alienation from people in general, regardless of their patienthood (for a more detailed description as well as supporting evidence see Chapter 4).

TABLE 13

Attitude Items that Correlated Significantly with Ward, Work, and Off-Ward Socializing Time

ITEM	WARD	WORK	OFF-WARD SOCIALIZING
1. It is a good thing to treat mental patients with kindness, but it probably will not do much toward helping them get well.	.51*	—.04	—.40*
2. Watching television is good therapy for a patient.	.47*	—.01	—.03
3. It would be hard to develop a close friendship with a person who has been a patient in a mental hospital.	.45*	—.06	—.42*
4. Every mental hospital should be surrounded by a high fence and guards.	.38*	.01	—.42*
5. A patient cannot get well unless he is prepared to suffer from his mental illness.	.37*	—.06	—.14
6. All patients in mental hospitals should be prevented from having children by a painless operation.	.35*	.14	—.43*
7. Once a mental patient, always a mental patient.	.35*	.12	—.47*
8. Patients will feel better if the hospital does not make any demands.	.31*	.28*	—.25
9. Regardless of how you look at it, patients with severe mental illness are no longer really human.	.29*	—.11	—.27*
10. The best way to handle patients in mental hospitals is to keep them behind locked doors.	.27*	.03	—.29*
11. There is little that can be done for mental patients in a mental hospital except to see that they are comfortable and well fed.	.27*	.34*	—.41*

TABLE 13 (continued)

ITEM	WARD	WORK	OFF-WARD SOCIALIZING
12. Medication is more helpful to a patient than individual or group therapy.	.27*	.02	—.39*
13. People who were once patients in mental hospitals are no more dangerous than the average citizen.	—.31*	.06	.09
14. The best doctors and drugs cannot cure a mental patient unless the patient does everything he can do to help himself.	—.26*	.08	.26*
15. The best way to fit into hospital life is to try to have a good time.	—.25	.01	.27*
16. If you want to, it is kind of easy to feel that you are not a patient in a hospital.	—.35*	.31*	.06
17. The best way to learn about the hospital is to ask patients who have been there for some time.	—.28*	.28*	.05
18. It is important to learn all about the hospital if you want to get things done and enjoy yourself.	—.25	.29*	.04
19. A woman would be foolish to marry a man who has a severe mental illness, even though he seems fully recovered.	—.11	.40*	—.29*
20. Better not to make many friends with patients while you are in the hospital.	.13	.36*	—.34*
21. Patients should be permitted to go into town whenever they wish to.	—.16	.35*	—.01
22. Patients would get better if the staff did not bother them.	.01	.34*	—.11
23. Patients should be required to work at a job while they are in the hospital.	—.02	.32*	—.18

TABLE 13 (continued)

ITEM	WARD	WORK	OFF-WARD SOCIALIZING
24. Patients should have more to say as to whether they should leave or stay in the hospital.	—.13	.31*	—.05
25. The administrators of mental hospitals should make a strong effort to hire staff members who are able to get along with people.	—.11	.30*	.30*
26. Although patients discharged from mental hospitals may seem alright, they should not be allowed to marry.	—.01	.30*	—.35*
27. If you want to get well again it is important to establish a comfortable routine in the hospital.	—.27*	.26*	.03
28. There are many people on the outside more disturbed than a lot of Old-timers in the hospital.	—.05	—.27*	.31*
29. A patient would be foolish not to try to enjoy himself as long as he is in the hospital.	—.20	—.18	.36*
30. Many people in our society are lonely and unrelated to their fellow human beings.	—.13	—.09	.32*
31. More tax money should be spent in the care and treatment of people with severe mental illness.	—.12	—.15	.28*
32. Sometimes an aide can be more important in making your stay in the hospital more comfortable than a doctor.	—.19	.01	.27*
33. Anyone who is in a hospital for mental illness should not be allowed to vote.	.10	.12	—.38*
34. The main purpose of a mental hospital should be to protect the public from a mentally ill person.	.08	.15	—.37*

TABLE 13 (continued)

ITEM	WARD	WORK	OFF-WARD SOCIALIZING
35. Even if a person who has been a patient in a mental hospital seems fully recovered, he should not be given a driver's license.	.06	.21	−.27*

*p > .01

Hypothesis 4: Styles of adaptation are significantly related to length of hospitalization.

Five months after the patients had been tested and interviewed, we determined whether or not they had been discharged. During this period, 34 patients had been discharged and 66 remained. Point biserial correlations were computed between staying and leaving and time spent on the ward, at work, and off the ward socializing. The correlations were: ward time and discharge, $r = .02$ (n.s.); work time and discharge, $r = -.46$ ($p < .001$); off-ward socializing and discharge, $r = .27$ ($p < .01$). If, however, we control for length of hospitalization at the time of testing, the correlation between off-ward socializing and discharge is significantly reduced ($r = .14$, n.s.), while the correlation between work and discharge is not significantly diminished ($r = -.35$, $p < .01$). Thus, when length of hospitalization is held constant, the only significant predictor of discharge is work time.

When the data are examined cross-sectionally, we find that length of hospitalization is related positively to the number of hours spent working ($r = .42$, $p < .001$), negatively to off-ward socializing ($r = -.39$, $p < .001$), and unrelated to ward time ($r = -.11$). The longer patients have been in the hospital, the more time they spend working and the less time off the wards socializing.

The results of both the longitudinal and cross-sectional analyses clearly suggest that patients who become "workers" early in their hospital life remain hospitalized for longer periods than those who become "warders" or "mobile socializers." A residue population of "workers," therefore, builds up in the hospital, representing the predominant, stable patient culture. This was made clear in the analysis of the 65 patients who manifested "pure" styles of adaptation. Sixty percent of the "mobile socializers" were discharged; 29 percent of the "warders"; and only 15 percent of the "workers" ($x^2 = 10.66$, $p < .01$). The selective migration holds up even when the Old-timers (patients who have been in the hospital four years or more) alone are examined. In this group ($N = 33$), 62 percent of the "mobile socializers" were discharged; 16 percent of the "warders"; and only 8 percent of the "workers" ($x^2 = 8.17$, $p < .02$). In short, then, Hypothesis 4 was confirmed.

Hypothesis 5: Adaptation styles are not related to indexes of patient psychopathology or hospital demands.

In the preceding study we demonstrated that diagnostic categories and premorbidity scores (Phillips, 1953) were not related to patient attitudes, information acquisition, or discharge rates. These findings were replicated in this study: neither the gross diagnostic breakdowns (such as schizophrenia versus nonschizophrenia) nor the finer subunits (such as paranoid schizophrenia versus chronic-undifferentiated schizophrenia) were related to patient attitudes, information, discharge, or styles of adaptation. Marital status, which correlated .87 with the Phillips' scores, was also unrelated to these variables.

The relationship between hospital demands made on patients and their styles of adaptation was insignificant, primarily because of minimal hospital intervention. Most patients were required to spend only half an hour (median) a day in hospital-directed locations, with the upper limit being two hours.

In addition, to the question "Where *can't* you spend time in the hospital?" 41 percent mentioned work areas such as offices; 39 percent stated that they did not know of any off-limit areas within the hospital grounds; 15 percent said that "leaving" the grounds was off-limits; and only 7 percent perceived restrictions within the living areas of the hospital. The question "Where *can* patients spend time in the hospital?" elicited a total of 70 different locations in the hospital. From the vantage point of the patient, then, the hospital not only restricts minimally their motility and free life space but also offers a "rich" milieu for alternative modes of adaptation.

We can conclude, then, that different styles of adaptation are unrelated both to hospital demands and to patient psychopathology; our hypothesis, here too, was supported.

Hypothesis 6: Styles of adaptation are significantly related to the patients' therapeutic involvements in the hospital.

Pointbiserial correlations were computed between ward, work, and off-ward socializing time and whether a patient ever had participated in psychotherapy (individual or group). Ward time, not surprisingly, was negatively related to entrance into psychotherapy ($r = -.27$, $p < .01$); off-ward socializing was positively related ($r = .30$, $p < .01$); and worktime was unrelated ($r = -.08$, n.s.).

Patient involvement in individual or group therapy was also associated with information acquisition. The correlation between HIT ratio scores and psychotherapy participation was $-.40$ ($p < .01$). More specifically, acquiring information about the staff was associated with having at some time been in therapy. In terms of absolute information scores, psychotherapy correlated .30 ($p < .01$) with residential information acquisition and .50 ($p < .01$) with hospital staff information. That is, patients who had been in psychotherapy knew more about the hospital in general and in particular more about the hospital staff than patients who had not participated in therapy. The results, therefore, strongly support Hypothesis 6.

DISCUSSION

To summarize our findings, three major styles of adaptation were identified: the "warders," the "workers," and the "mobile socializers." Each of these styles is associated with a different kind of patient (differentiated as to age, kinds of attitudes held about hospitalization, patienthood, goals, and interests); as we anticipated, each led to different hospital outcomes (namely, information acquired, length of hospitalization, discharge rates, and therapeutic involvement). Moreover, these styles of adaptation were unrelated to indexes of psychopathology and to direct hospital pressures.

These results clearly support our assertion that hospitalized mental patients can be understood in terms usually reserved for normals. The same constructs and assumptions employed in understanding the interaction between normal people and their communities also can be used to understand the relationship between mental patients and their community, the mental hospital. These relationships were predicted by a model that made no recourse to assumptions concerning the dynamics of psychopathology or institutional power.

Indeed, the findings did not offer any evidence for the traditional belief that mental patients are functionally different from people in general, particularly in the sense that they are more helpless and less able to control their fate than their nonhospitalized counterparts. To the contrary, the results show that mental patients are successful in utilizing their environment to their satisfaction; that they can and do initiate and maintain the life styles they value, even when these styles depart from those valued by the institution.

We have, thus far, uncovered two rather illuminating facets about mental patients and how they live in the hospital. First, we have shown that mental patients are effective human beings, capable of employing subtle forms of counterpower (impression management) in order to meet their needs, and second, that they can live the kind of life they desire within the confines of an institution. We consider these findings important because they generate a kind of insight precluded by the psychiatric perspective that now enables us to more accurately understand observations concerning mental patients.

It has always been known that there are certain patients (usually called "backward" or "regressed schizophrenics") who are invisible to the psychiatry staff. Hospital psychiatrists are the first to admit that they do not know all of their many patients. It is generally believed that this type of patient is avoided by the psychiatrists and, as a result, fades more or less into obscurity. This phenomenon has been attributed to the psychiatrists' lack of interest in some patients, because they are somehow unreachable, and therefore, untreatable (Stanton and Schwartz, 1954). More specifically, it is the traditional belief of psychiatrists that chronic schizophrenics are in some way deficient (symbolically, chemically, interpersonally) and that their illness imposes social isolation. Thus, it is the patient's disease rather than the patient himself that facilitates the psychiatrist's avoidance and, ultimately, the patient's invisibility.

In the light not only of our theoretical position but of the five preceding studies as well, this explanation or, rather, pseudo-explanation seems grossly inadequate. We agree, of course, that patients do vary with respect to their visibility. We do not believe, however, that they acquire high or low visibility out of default to their illness or to the psychiatrist's reaction to their illness. Our model, instead, would view patient invisibility as a desired outcome of their system of motives, which is achieved by means of their style of adaptation to the hospital.

In order to test our assumptions as well as to demonstrate once more the heuristic value of our model, a final study was conducted by B. Braginsky, D. Braginsky and K. Ring.

THE INVISIBLE MENTAL PATIENT: A FATE OR A WAY OF LIFE?

From our point of view, patients' styles of adaptation based on their long-standing motivational states, determine how much contact they have with their psychiatrist, which, in turn, influences their invisibility status. For instance, if a patient wants to stay in the hospital, a successful strategy would be to avoid his doctor and thereby minimize his visibility. Surely, an invisible patient would not be discharged. Or, if a patient wants to have a good time while he is in the hospital (that is, to avoid therapy programs and to participate mainly in recreational and social activities), he too would be wise to avoid the psychiatrists (assuming here that contact with psychiatrists maximizes the chance of being assigned to therapy programs).

In short, we believe that patient visibility is primarily a function of the patients' motives and styles of adaptation rather than an outcome of their pathology.

METHOD

Ten psychiatrists (eight men and two women) were asked to try to recall the names of all the patients assigned to them ($N = 281$). Then, within a three-day interval, they were presented with a list of the names of their patients and were asked to recall each patient's age (within ten years), length of hospitalization, and diagnosis and to give a brief description of what the patient did with his time in the hospital. In addition each patient was rated on two dimensions: (a) patient-initiated contact with the psychiatrist, on a five-point scale ranging from "very actively approaches his psychiatrist" (5) to "very actively avoids his psychiatrist" (1) and (b) the actual amount of contact the psychiatrist had with the patient, on a five-point scale ranging from "a great deal of contact" (5) to "little or no contact" (1).

From the 281 patients, a subgroup of 60 (30 men and 30 women) were randomly selected from the rosters, with an equal number of recalled and unrecalled patients for each psychiatrist. The style of adaptation was determined for each of the 60 patients on the basis of an interview (see page 98). Demographic information was obtained as well as follow-up data regarding discharge.

SUBJECTS   The mean age of the 60 subjects was 45.6 years, with a standard deviation of 12.1. Their mean educational level was 10.2 years, with a standard deviation of 2.8. Their median length of hospitalization was eight years. Ninety-two percent of the sample were diagnosed as schizophrenic and the remaining 8 percent as nonpsychotic. There were no significant differences between male and female patients on these variables.

DESIGN AND HYPOTHESES   Subjects in our subanalysis were classified according to sex and visibility or invisibility (recalled or not recalled), thus giving us a two-by-two factorial design. There were 15 Ss in each of the four cells.

Our hypotheses are based on the model of styles of adaptation presented earlier (see page 78). They are: (1) Patients vary in their degree of visibility to their psychiatrist. (2) Patient visibility is an outcome of and, therefore, significantly related to patient approach or avoidance behavior rather than psychiatrist approach or avoidance behavior. (3) Patients' approach or avoidance behavior is significantly related to their styles of adaptation. (4) Visibility is *not* related to indexes of patient psychopathology.

RESULTS AND DISCUSSION

The data obtained from the psychiatrists showed that they recalled, on the average, 57.6 percent of their patients; the range was from 12 percent to 87 percent. The differences were related to the size of each psychiatrist's group; those with larger groups remembered fewer patients. There were no systematic differences in recall with respect to the sex of the psychiatrist or the sex of the patient. The psychiatrist's later responses to the patient rosters, however, indicated that they were very accurate with respect to recalling patients' diagnoses, age, and length of hospitalization. With the exception of the working patients, the psychiatrists said they had no idea of how their patients typically spent their time in the hospital!

Table 14 presents the mean approach scores for the visible and invisible male and female patients. The analysis of variance of these data showed that females approach the psychiatrists more than males ($F = 35.95$, $p < .001$) and that the visible patients approach the doctors significantly more than the invisible ones ($F = 8.84$, $p < .01$).

TABLE 14

*Mean Patient Approach-Avoidance Scores**

	VISIBLE	INVISIBLE	TOTAL MEAN
Males	2.40	2.00	2.20
Females	3.21	2.80	3.01
TOTAL MEAN	2.81	2.40	

*High scores indicate approach (5); low scores, avoidance (1).

With respect to the frequency of contact, the psychiatrists reported that they had more contact with female than with male patients ($F = 19.48$, $p < .001$) and that they had significantly more contact with the patients whom they recalled earlier than those whom they did not ($F = 15.96$, $p < .001$). These means, presented in Table 15, also indicate an interaction between sex and visibility, but this interaction is a function primarily of the great amount of contact women have with their psychiatrists.

TABLE 15

Mean Frequency of Patient-Psychiatrist Contact

	VISIBLE	INVISIBLE	TOTAL MEAN
Males	2.75	1.52	2.04
Females	3.14	2.83	2.99
TOTAL MEAN	2.95	2.18	

To the extent that the actual amount of contact is related to the patients' approaching their psychiatrist, we can determine the relative influence of the psychiatrist with respect to patient-doctor interactions. That is, if we find that patients who have a great deal of contact with their psychiatrist are the ones who initiate the interaction (actively approach) and that those who have little or no contact are the "avoiders," then we may presume that the role of the psychiatrist here is minimal. This, in fact, was the case; the correlation between patient approach and amount of contact ($N = 235$) was .60 ($p < .001$), giving further support to our assertion that patients are active and effective in determining their degree of visibility.

Because we have demonstrated that mental patients vary in their degree of visibility and that this variance is a perceived function of their, rather than the psychiatrist's, approach or avoidance behavior, Hypotheses 1 and 2 stand confirmed.

The questions that remain concern the characteristics and styles of adaptation of the visible and invisible patients. In order to provide some answers, detailed analyses were conducted on the subgroup of 60 patients.

As one might expect, the invisible patients were those who had been in and probably want to remain in the hospital for long periods. That is, those who were visible had an average stay of 5.3 years while the invisible patients were in the hospital on the average of 7.3 years ($F = 5.94$, $p < .05$). Because we have already shown that length of hospitalization is unrelated to indexes of severity of psychopathology, a pathology interpretation appears somewhat inadequate. More direct evidence for this point will be presented shortly.

The three aspects of adaptation styles, ward, work, and off-ward socializing were examined next. Table 16 presents the mean hours of time spent on the ward for the four groups. As one can readily see, women spend significantly more time on the ward than men ($F = 26.01$, $p < .001$). In addition, visibility interacts with sex ($F = 13.06$, $p < .001$); visible men spend significantly less time on the ward than the three other groups, whereas visible women spend significantly more time on the ward than the others. This interaction, though at first puzzling, becomes more meaningful when the ward activities of men and women are compared. As we shall demonstrate shortly, men spending time on the ward typically engage in nonsocial activities (for example, sitting alone or reading), whereas women on the ward spend most of their time socializing. Thus, women who flit around socializing attain greater visibility than the men, who prefer to sit quietly minding their own business.

TABLE 16

Mean Number of Hours Spent on the Ward

	VISIBLE	INVISIBLE	TOTAL MEAN
Males	4.57	7.60	6.09
Females	10.33	8.07	9.20
TOTAL MEAN	7.45	7.84	

Table 17 presents the mean hours spent working. The analysis of variance of these data[29] indicated, again, a significant interaction between sex and visibility ($F = 43.04$, $p < .001$). That is, visible women spent significantly less time working than the three other groups.

TABLE 17

Mean Number of Hours Spent at Work

	VISIBLE	INVISIBLE	TOTAL MEAN
Males	2.77	3.13	2.95
Females	1.10	2.30	1.70
TOTAL MEAN	1.94	2.72	

Time spent off the ward socializing, the means of which are presented in Table 18, also yielded a significant sex by visibility interaction ($F = 16.60$, $p < .001$). More specifically, visible men spent significantly more time off the ward socializing than any other group, and invisible women spent more time at this than

TABLE 18

Mean Number of Hours Spent off the Ward Socializing

	VISIBLE	INVISIBLE	TOTAL MEAN
Males	6.10	2.50	4.30
Females	1.90	3.17	2.54
TOTAL MEAN	4.00	2.84	

[29]A logarithmic transformation was used for these data because many of the patients did not work at all (scores of zero).

visible women. In addition, a significant main effect for sex emerged; men spent more time at off-ward socializing than women ($F = 8.75$, $p < .01$).

Thus, there seem to be different strategies for patients to attain either visibility or invisibility depending upon their sex. For women, in order to assure invisibility, the best strategy appears to be to stay off the ward, either in social activities or at work; the best assurance for men, however, is to stay quietly on the ward. It also seems clear that it is the "typical" or modal patient who is most readily recalled. That is, the norm for women patients is to be "homebodies" (to stay close to the ward), while for men the norm is to get out and work or socialize off the ward. The "atypical" men (the homebodies) and the "atypical" women (the workers and off-ward socializers) are the least visible patients.

Of course, if one wished, he could still cling to the belief that the invisible patients are in fact more severely disturbed and that the atypicality merely reflects the degree of psychopathology. In order to strengthen our contradictory assertion, then, two further analyses were conducted.

A comparison was made between the visible and invisible patients with respect to diagnostic categories. The results indicated no significant differences between the groups, although, admittedly, these data were somewhat restricted (92 percent of the patients had been diagnosed as schizophrenic).

So that we might directly counter the psychopathology argument, especially the assertion that the patients who are perceived by their psychiatrist as being severely ill are avoided by him and, therefore, become invisible, the following procedure was employed. Several months after the psychiatrists participated in the study, two of the ten were asked to rate on a five-point scale the severity of illness for 66 of their patients who were in the original sample. A score of 5 indicated a slight degree of pathology and a score of 1, a high degree.

The means for the visible ($N = 37$) and invisible ($N = 29$) patients were 2.81 ($SD = 1.16$) and 2.79 ($SD = 1.09$), respectively. Obviously, the difference between them was insignificant. In addition, a chi-square analysis, using a "very sick" (scores of 1 and 2) and a "hardly sick" (4 and 5) split, also yielded insignificant results.

It is clear that visibility is unrelated to how disturbed or healthy a patient appears to be to his psychiatrist.

Earlier we asserted that invisibility was very much in keeping with the *desire* to remain hospitalized. In order to test this hypothesis, five-month follow-up data concerning discharge were collected. Using only the patients who at the time of testing had been hospitalized for eight years or less[30] ($N = 32$), we found that 42 percent of the visible patients had been discharged, whereas only 8 percent of the invisible patients had been released ($x^2 = 4.52$, $p < .05$). Our assertion therefore appears valid.

To summarize, the findings in this study supported our hypotheses:

1. Patients do vary with respect to their visibility.

2. This variability was a function of perceived patient-initiated approach or avoidance of their psychiatrist.

3. Visibility was significantly related to styles of adaptation, although somewhat differently for men and women. Visible men spent less time on the ward and more time off the ward socializing than the invisible men; visible women, on the other hand, spent more time on the ward (socializing there) and less time off the ward at either work or social activities than the women who were invisible.

4. Visibility was unrelated to psychiatrists' ratings of patient psychopathology.

5. More visible patients are discharged than invisible patients.

All of our research so far has considered only individual differences among patients, although we have at times implied certain similarities (for example, hedonic attitudes of patients). But surely, if we adhere to our assumption that mental patients are similar to people in general, we should expect to find similarities among them just as we expect to find similarities among people in any given community. It would be enlightening, therefore, to present a portrayal of the "national character" of mental patients. That is, over and above individual variation, what are the beliefs, attitudes, interests, styles of adaptation of the *modal* mental patient?[31]

[30]This cut-off point was chosen because none of the patients in our sample who were hospitalized for nine or more years ($N = 25$) were discharged.
[31]The term *modal* is emphasized because we are not concerned with the statistically average patient but rather with the charactristics most patients share.

THE MODAL MENTAL PATIENT

Because we have relevant data available from the studies presented earlier (see especially, the section in this chapter entitled "Patient Styles of Adaptation to a Mental Hospital"), we will spare the reader a repetition of the procedural details and will examine directly the modal patient's information acquisition, attitudes, therapeutic involvement, and styles of adaptation.

INFORMATION ACQUISITION

Table 19 presents the percentage of correct responses to the Hospital Information Test items ($N = 100$). Clearly, more patients have information about the residential aspects of the hospital than they do about the hospital staff. For example, 78 percent knew where the hospital post office and garage were lo-

TABLE 19

Percentage of Correct Responses to HIT
Items (N = 100)

ITEMS	PERCENT CORRECT
1. Number of floors in patient's unit	84
2. Location of the bowling alley	82
3. Location of gym	80
4. Location of swimming pool	80
5. Location of hospital post office	78
6. Location of hospital garage	78
7. Location of patient dances	70
8. Name of the movie theater building	70
9. Name of the building the canteen is in	68
10. Number and times of nursing shifts	64
11. Publication times of the hospital magazine	64

TABLE 19 (continued)

ITEMS	PERCENT CORRECT
12. Location of the main dental office	63
13. Where good used clothing is located	62
14. Name of the hospital magazine	62
15. Location of the nursing supervisor's office	60
16. Location of the gift shop	60
17. Name of the nursing supervisor	59
18. Number of patients in the subject's unit	58
19. Number of libraries in hospital	56
20. Name of medication patient receives	54
21. Location of the police department	54
22. Location of the hospital switchboard	54
23. Location of the out-patient clinic	52
24. Location of the printing shop	50
25. Location of the libraries	50
26. Amount of vacation time state employees receive	50
27. Name of subject's psychiatrist	48
28. Location of the shoe repair shop	48
29. Location of the laboratory	48
30. Name of the superintendent	46
31. Name of the OT building	46
32. Location of the school	46
33. Location of the psychology department	46
34. Knowledge of visiting days	44
35. Number of patients in the hospital	44
36. Name of the medical and surgical building	44

TABLE 19 (continued)

ITEMS	PERCENT CORRECT
37. Name of the doctor in charge of subject's building	42
38. Name of used clothes shop	42
39. Location of the tailor shop	42
40. Location of the superintendent's office	40
41. Location of the hospital pharmacy	40
42. Names of the buildings employees live in	40
43. Name of the chapel	40
44. Knowledge of visiting hours	40
45. Location of office of subject's doctor	38
46. Knowledge of library hours	38
47. Location of psychologist's office	36
48. Location of the music department	34
49. Location of nurse's office	34
50. Name of a nurse in subject's building	34
51. Location of the business manager's office	30
52. Name of a psychologist in subject's building	26
53. Name of a social worker in subject's building	26
54. Name of a nursing supervisor in other buildings	24
55. Location of social worker's office	22
56. Name of the business manager	22
57. Name of a nurse in other buildings	20
58. Location of head of volunteer's office	18
59. Knowledge of own diagnosis	16
60. Name of head of nursing department	15
61. Name of a doctor in charge in other buildings	14

TABLE 19 (continued)

ITEMS	PERCENT CORRECT
62. Name of the head of OT department	14
63. Name of the head of social service department	12
64. Name of a psychiatrist in other buildings	12
65. Name of the head of volunteers	10
66. Name of a social worker in other buildings	6
67. Name of a psychologist in other buildings	2

cated, while only 48 percent knew the name of their own psychiatrist. In addition, the hedonic quality to which we have often
alluded is reflected in the types of locations most of the patients
knew. Although only 38 percent knew the location of their own
doctor's office and 46 percent knew the whereabouts of the occupational therapy building, 82 percent knew where to find the
bowling alley, 80 percent knew the location of the gym and
swimming pool, and 70 percent knew where the movies were
shown and dances were held.

PATIENT ATTITUDES

Here modal patient beliefs are defined as at least 70 percent
patient agreement (scale responses of 4, 5, or 6) or 70 percent
disagreement (scale responses of 1, 2, or 3) on the PAT (Patient
Attitude Test) items. These are presented in Table 20. A perusal
of this table indicates that (1) patients desire a comfortable, enjoyable, nondemanding, laissez-faire milieu in the hospital; (2)
they do not perceive themselves as particularly mentally ill or
different from nonhospitalized persons; (3) they perceive themselves as capable of controlling entry to and exit from the hospital;
(4) they want to maintain the civil and social rights they had
prior to becoming mental patients; and (5) they do not perceive
the hospital as being very dissimilar from outside communities.

TABLE 20

Modal Patient Attitudes
(N = 100)

AGREE

1. A patient would be foolish not to try to enjoy himself as long as he is in the hospital.

2. In many ways a hospital is just like any other neighborhood you find on the outside.

3. The best way to fit into hospital life is to try to have a good time.

4. If you really want to, it is not too hard to stay or leave the hospital.

5. It's possible to have a good and full life in the hospital while you are a patient.

6. There are many people on the outside more disturbed than a lot of Old-timers in the hospital.

7. It's good therapy to spend most of your time relaxing and enjoying your stay in the hospital.

8. A patient should try to make his life as simple as possible while in the hospital.

9. The patients in mental hospitals should have something to say about the way the hospital is run.

10. It's important to learn all about the hospital if you want to get things done and enjoy yourself.

11. When a person has a problem or worry, it is best not to think about it, but keep busy with more pleasant things.

12. All most patients need is a period of relaxation to get on their feet again.

13. A patient should not think about leaving but rather how he can get well again.

14. If you want to get well again, it is important to establish a comfortable routine in the hospital.

15. A patient should never leave the hospital until he is completely cured.

16. Patients will feel better if the hospital does not make any demands.

17. Everything a person does in the hospital, including having coffee in the canteen, is therapeutic.

TABLE 20 (continued)

AGREE

18. You should always do what the staff wants you to even if you disagree with them.

19. Watching television is good therapy for a patient.

20. A patient should try to meet as many other patients as possible rather than to limit himself to patients on his own ward.

21. You should try to be on friendly terms with the staff on the ward.

22. A hospital should not ask a patient to do what he had not done on the outside.

23. The administrators of mental hospitals should make a strong effort to hire staff members who are able to get along with people.

DISAGREE

1. Although patients discharged from mental hospitals may seem all right, they should not be allowed to marry.

2. The best way to handle patients in mental hospitals is to keep them behind locked doors.

3. Regardless of how you look at it, patients with severe mental illness are no longer really human.

4. Once a mental patient, always a mental patient.

5. All patients in mental hospitals should be prevented from having children by a painless operation.

6. An employer would be foolish to hire a person who has been a patient in a mental hospital, even if he seems fully recovered and is well trained for the job.

7. It is a good thing to treat mental patients with kindness, but it probably will not do much toward helping them get well.

8. Even if a person who has been a patient in a mental hospital seems fully recovered, he should not be given a driver's license.

9. I don't think there should be mental hospitals but rather only out-patient clinics.

10. A woman would be foolish to marry a man who has had a severe mental illness, even though he seems fully recovered.

11. Anyone who is in a hospital for mental illness should not be allowed to vote.

12. Every mental hospital should be surrounded by a high fence and guards.

TABLE 20 (continued)

DISAGREE

---

13. The law should allow a woman to divorce her husband as soon as he has been confined in a mental hospital with a severe mental illness.

14. A patient cannot get well unless he is prepared to suffer from his illness.

15. It is better not to make friends with patients while you are in the hospital.

THERAPEUTIC INVOLVEMENT

At the time the patients were tested, only 10 of the 100 were involved in individual or group psychotherapy, while 30 were in occupational therapy programs. All 40 patients reported that they had been assigned to rather than volunteered for these programs. In addition 32 patients reported that at some time during their hospital stay they had been in individual or group psychotherapy. The median length of time spent in such contacts was, however, only four weeks, with no patient reporting having spent more than two months in *any* form of psychotherapy. Thus it seems fair to conclude that their therapeutic involvement is considerably less than the hospital staff might desire.

STYLES OF ADAPTATION

The means for time spent on the ward, at work, and in recreational areas off the ward were, respectively. 7.50 hours ($SD = 3.01$), 2.21 hours ($SD = 2.85$), and 3.11 hours ($SD = 2.95$). The modal patient, then, spends most of his time on the ward, and when off the ward he spends more time in recreational areas than at work.

It should be noted, however, that men and women, while on the ward, engage in very different activities. The most frequently mentioned activities reported by male patients were watching TV (92 percent), reading (83 percent), sitting alone (54 percent), playing cards (44 percent), and conversation with other patients (35 percent). Women, on the other hand, spent most of their time on the ward in conversation with other patients (62 percent), and when they were not socially engaged they tended to sit alone (45 percent).

When patients were off the ward and were not at work, they typically frequented the recreation rooms (86 percent), the canteens (85 percent), the gym (64 percent), other wards (62 percent), hospital grounds (60 percent), and building lobbies (58 percent). The patients who spent their time working had essentially unskilled but indispensable hospital jobs, such as cafeteria work, laundry, and garbage collection. Seventy percent of the working patients volunteered for these assignments, which, for the most part, took the patients off their own wards (85 percent of the jobs were off the patient's ward).

When one looks at how patients spend their time in the hospital, what they learn about it, what their attitudes are, and the extent of their therapeutic involvement, the results are, to say the least, edifying. Mental patients typically manifest a lack of therapeutic involvement; maintain attitudes that stress strivings for a comfortable, nondemanding, laissez-faire hospital existence; do not perceive themselves as particularly ill, helpless, or different from other people and acquire more information about the residential aspects of the institution rather than the hospital staff or therapeutic facilities. This picture is a far cry from the way in which most professionals view the typical mental patient. Thus, the typical patient attitudes, needs, interests, and the resultant styles of adaptation that we suggested earlier have been substantiated by the data.

We have shown, in any case, not only that hospital demands are minimal, but also that the institution offers to the patients many alternative avenues for adaptation. That patients can and do take advantage of these alternatives in a way that satisfies their system of motives also was demonstrated. Thus, we feel that at least we have eliminated and rendered untenable the notions that patients, when confronted by the institution, are impotent and powerless and that they are basically frightened, inadequate, acquiescent people. These data taken as a whole cannot be accounted for (either predicted or adequately explained) by any of the conventional psychological or sociological theories dealing with mental patients and mental institutions. These assumptions have been replaced by others that are clearly of great value with respect to understanding not only the nature of the mental patient but also the relationship between the patient and the institution.

We have not, however, examined one major assertion underlying our model: namely, that the style of adaptation a mental patient exhibits in the hospital is consistent with and in most ways identical to his style of adaptation to the community at large.

We now turn, therefore, to studies that examine the patient's style of adaptation prior to hospitalization and that offer more direct evidence to substantiate our assumption about the continuity of the pre- and posthospital life styles.

CHAPTER
4

The Last Resort

Unlike life in the mental hospital, leisure time in the outside community is a special event: nonhospitalized citizens have to wait for weekends, holidays, and vacations to taste the fruits of minimal environmental demands. The mental patient, however, finds himself more than adequately blessed with this luxury—in the mental hospital free time is the rule. Most patients are in a somewhat advantageous and perhaps envious position, for not only are they free to choose a style of adaptation that most suits their needs but also they find themselves as select members of a leisure class.

Chapter 3 has already demonstrated the efficacious use patients make of the hospital. It has not been demonstrated, however, whether the life styles established in the hospital are peculiar to that setting or are, in fact, direct extensions of the patients' prehospital, community styles of life. The significance of this question is twofold. First, if our model of social adaptation is appropriate for mental patients, we should find a continuity between how patients adapt to the hospital and how they adapted to the community. That is, if patients are like people in general, they should be able to transport "old" but preferred styles of adaptation into new settings. Second, if we find that patients use leisure time (an everyday event) in the hospital in the same fashion that they had used their leisure time in the community (a special weekend event), we must redefine the primary functions of the mental hospital. In this case the mental hospital could be viewed as an extension of the patient's "old hunting grounds" and the patient seen as a person who primarily spends his time as if he were on a "long weekend"—not only in the sense of time but also in the spirit of the pursuit of pleasure. Thus, for most patients the hospital could no longer be assumed to have a solely educative, therapeutic, or even custodial relevancy (Levinson and Gallagher, 1964). Instead, we would have to view the relationship between the patient and the hospital as a function of a hedonistic calculus where the hospital is to be seen as a potential pleasure dome and the patient as an architect of his own personal Shangri-La. Evidence has already been adduced (see Chapter 3) demonstrating the patients' hedonistic attitudes and styles of adaptation. What remains to be seen is whether these styles of adaptation and the goals they satisfy are simply extensions of prehospital "weekend" ways of life. A study, therefore, was conducted by B. Braginsky, J. Holzberg, D. Braginsky, H. Arbor, and K. Ring.

THE RELATIONSHIP BETWEEN COMMUNITY AND HOSPITAL STYLES OF ADAPTATION

We believe that patients, as most people, when given the opportunity to structure their own time with minimal interference from external sources, will structure it in a way that is maximally compatible with their needs. Because the period of minimal external demands in the community is on weekends, but in the hospital every day, we predict that a more positive relationship exists between the patient's former weekend rather than weekday style of adaptation and his present everyday style of life in the hospital.

METHOD

The procedure here involved similar questionnaire surveys and interviews to those used in our studies of adaptation styles in the mental hospital. There were, however, some important methodological differences. First, our sample was composed of first admissions to a mental hospital. This allowed us to eliminate the possible interactions that may occur between prior hospitalization experiences, styles of adaptation in a subsequent rehospitalization, and posthospital adaptation to the community. Second, subjects were tested immediately upon entry to the hospital. This assured us that the patient had not as yet entered the mainstream of hospital life. The attitudes we assessed, then, represented those that patients carried into the hospital rather than ones that the patients had derived from their experiences in the hospital. Patients were tested in the following manner.

FIRST TESTING SESSION (IMMEDIATELY UPON ENTRY TO THE HOSPITAL)

Community Styles of Adaptation Patients were asked to give a detailed hourly account of where and how they spent their waking time during a "typical" 24-hour day during weekdays in the community. In addition, they were asked to give the same detailed report about their activities on weekends. Each patient was then assigned three scores for weekdays and three scores for weekends. They were the number of hours spent at home, at work, and out of home at informal social activities. As in our earlier study of styles of adaptation to the hospital, the categories accounted for almost all of the patients' responses.

Patient Attitude Test (PAT) All subjects were individually administered the PAT.

Phillips Premorbid Adjustment Scale The Phillips scale, a measure of premorbid social skills and competency was also individually administered during the testing session.

Demographic Measures Information about age, education, diagnostic status, type of admission, employment history, and affiliation with patients and/or former mental patients was obtained for all subjects.

SECOND TESTING SESSION (THREE WEEKS AFTER
ADMISSION)

Hospital Styles of Adaptation   The identical procedure described in Chapter 3 (see page 98) was used in order to obtain information as to how patients adapted to the hospital.

Patient Attitude Test   Patients were also readministered the PAT.

SUBJECTS   One hundred twenty-five subjects (78 men and 47 women) were tested during a six-month period. The mean age was 30.8 years with a standard deviation of 11.5 years. The mean educational level was 10.7 years with a standard deviation of 2.4 years. The diagnostic category breakdown was 57 percent schizophrenic, 11 percent psychotic, and 32 percent nonpsychotic. The mean of the Phillips premorbid adjustment scale was 10.8 with a standard deviation of 7.6. Forty-one percent of the patients reported both having friends who were still or had been patients at the hospital and having discussed the hospital with the friends prior to admission.

RESULTS AND DISCUSSION

Hypothesis: A more positive relationship exists between the patient's former weekend rather than weekday style of adaptation and his present everyday style of life in the hospital.

To evaluate this hypothesis we considered the 48 subjects (28 men and 20 women) who were not discharged during the three-week interval between the first and second testing sessions. After they were tested for the second time, their prehospital or community styles of adaptation were correlated with their hospital styles of adaptation. The results were as follows: home time during weekends was significantly related to ward time ($r = .59$, $p < .001$) while home time during weekdays was not ($r = .23$, n.s.); both weekend and weekday socializing time were significantly related to off-ward socializing time, the correlations respectively were $r = .61$, $p < .001$, $r = .38$, $p < .01$. The correlation between home time during weekends and ward time was significantly higher ($p < .01$) than the correlation between weekday home time and ward time. Similarly, weekend socializing time was more significantly related to off-ward socializing time ($p < .05$) than was weekday socializing time. Correlations for work time could not be computed because only 4 out of the 48 patients held jobs in the hospital during the three-week period.

An analysis of diagnostic categories and Phillips scores with adaptation styles both in and out of the hospital revealed no significant relationships. Thus, the best predictor of patient adaptation to the hospital was not diagnostic categories nor premorbid scores nor even weekday community styles of adaptation but rather how patients spent their time during weekends in the community. It is noteworthy that prior to hospitalization 98 percent of the patients in this sample worked a full 40-hour week and that 30 percent worked more than 40 hours a week. Our sample, then, was not composed of mendicants or recluses but rather of people who were gainfully employed until the time of admission to the hospital. Thus weekends or leisure time for these people were in fact special and rare events. In summary, our hypothesis stands confirmed.

Another analysis, although not a direct test of our hypothesis, was conducted in order to determine whether a continuity existed between prehospital and hospital attitudes. In this analysis we compared the correlations between prehospital styles of adaptation and the 86 PAT items obtained from the 125 first-admission subjects with the corresponding correlations obtained from the 100 Old-timer patient sample (see Table 21).

The comparison shows that first-admission patients who were weekend homebodies in the community maintain similar attitudes about the hospital, patienthood, and mental illness to warders in the hospital; first-admission patients who were weekend mobile socializers in the community share similar attitudes with mobile socializers in the hospital; a slightly negative correspondence of attitudes exists, however, between weekend workers in the community and workers in the hospital. For the most part, adaptation styles in the hospital have the same attitudinal correlates as their weekend community counterparts, lending further evidence in support of our continuity hypothesis.

TABLE 21

A Comparison of the Attitudinal Correlates of Hospital and Community Styles of Adaptation

ITEM	HOME TIME	WARD TIME
1. It is a good thing to treat mental patients with kindness but it probably will not do much toward helping them get well.	.34	.51
2. Watching television is good therapy for a patient.	.31	.47
3. It would be hard to develop a close friendship with a person who has been a patient in a mental hospital.	.36	.45
4. Every mental hospital should be surrounded by a high fence and guards.	.31	.38
5. A patient cannot get well unless he is prepared to suffer from his illness.	.29	.36
6. All patients in mental hospitals should be prevented from having children by a painless operation.	.30	.35
7. Once a mental patient, always a mental patient.	.37	.35
8. Patients will feel better if the hospital does not make any demands.	.02	.31
9. Regardless of how you look at it, patients with severe mental illness are no longer really human.	.35	.29
10. The best way to handle patients in mental hospitals is to keep them behind locked doors.	.30	.27
11. There is little that can be done for mental patients in a mental hospital except to see that they are comfortable and well fed.	.36	.27

TABLE 21 (continued)

ITEM	HOME TIME	WARD TIME
12. Medication is more helpful to a patient than individual or group therapy.	.29	.27
13. People who were once patients in mental hospitals are no more dangerous than the average citizen.	—.35	—.31
14. The best doctors and drugs cannot cure a mental patient unless the patient does everything he can do to help himself.	—.25	—.26
15. If you want to, it is kind of easy to feel that you are not a patient in a hospital.	.15	—.35
16. The best way to learn about the hospital is to ask patients who have been there for some time.	—.06	—.29
17. If you want to get well again, it is important to establish a comfortable routine in the hospital.	.04	—.27

ITEM	COMMUNITY SOCIALIZING	HOSPITAL SOCIALIZING
1. It is a good thing to treat mental patients with kindness, but it probably will not do much toward helping them get well.	—.11	—.40
2. It would be hard to develop a close friendship with a person who has been a patient in a mental hospital.	—.37	—.42
3. Every mental hospital should be surrounded by a high fence and guards.	—.35	—.42
4. All patients in mental hospitals should be prevented from having children by a painless operation.	—.16	—.43

TABLE 21 (continued)

ITEM	COMMUNITY SOCIALIZING	HOSPITAL SOCIALIZING
5. Once a mental patient, always a mental patient.	−.17	−.47
6. Regardless of how you look at it, patients with severe mental illness are no longer really human.	−.29	−.27
7. There are many people on the outside more disturbed than a lot of Old-timers in the hospital.	.34	.31
8. A patient would be foolish not to try to enjoy himself as long as he is in the hospital.	.01	.36
9. Many people in our society are lonely and unrelated to their fellow human beings.	.39	.32
10. More tax money should be spent in the care and treatment of people with severe mental illness.	.26	.28
11. The best way to fit into hospital life is to try to have a good time.	.35	.27
12. Anyone who is in a hospital for mental illness should not be allowed to vote.	−.24	−.38
13. The main purpose of a mental hospital should be to protect the public from a mentally ill person.	−.16	−.37
14. Even if a person who has been a patient in a mental hospital seems fully recovered he should not be given a drivers license.	−.35	−.27
15. The best way to handle patients in mental hospitals is to keep them behind locked doors.	−.29	−.29
16. There is little than can be done for mental patients in a mental hospital except to see that they are comfortable and well fed.	−.48	−.41

TABLE 21 (continued)

ITEM	COMMUNITY SOCIALIZING	HOSPITAL SOCIALIZING
17. Medication is more helpful to a patient than individual or group therapy.	−.31	−.39
18. The best doctors and drugs cannot cure a mental patient unless the patient does everything he can do to help himself.	.14	.26
19. A woman would be foolish to marry a man who has a severe mental illness, even though he seems fully recovered.	−.37	−.29
20. It is better not to make friends with patients while you are in the hospital.	−.35	−.34
21. The administrators of mental hospitals should make a strong effort to hire staff members who are able to get along with people.	.23	.30
22. Although patients discharged from mental hospitals may seem all right, they should not be allowed to marry.	−.35	−.35

ITEM	COMMUNITY WORK TIME	HOSPITAL WORK TIME
1. Patients will feel better if the hospital does not make any demands.	−.30	.28
2. There are many people on the outside more disturbed than a lot of Old-timers in the hospital.	−.14	−.27
3. There is little that can be done for mental patients in a mental hospital except to see that they are comfortable and well fed.	−.07	.34
4. If you want to, it is kind of easy to feel that you are not a patient in a hospital.	−.32	.31

TABLE 21 (continued)

ITEM	COMMUNITY WORK TIME	HOSPITAL WORK TIME
5. The best way to learn about the hospital is to ask patients who have been there for some time.	—.34	.28
6. It is important to learn all about the hospital if you want to get things done and enjoy yourself.	—.28	.29
7. A woman would be foolish to marry a man who has a severe mental illness, even though he seems fully recovered.	—.07	.40
8. It is better not to make friends with patients while you are in the hospital.	—.20	.36
9. Patients should be permitted to go into town whenever they wish to.	—.15	.35
10. Patients would get better if the staff did not bother them.	—.06	.32
11. Patients should be required to work at a job while they are in the hospital.	.06	.32
12. Patients should have more to say as to whether they should leave or stay in the hospital.	—.34	.31
13. If you want to, it is kind of easy to feel that you are not a patient in a hospital.	.15	.31
14. The administrators of mental hospitals should make a strong effort to hire staff members who are able to get along with people.	—.10	.30
15. Although patients discharged from mental hospitals may seem all right, they should not be allowed to marry.	.03	.30
16. If you want to get well again it is important to establish a comfortable routine in the hospital.	—.10	.26

This evidence strongly suggests that patients do not have to be taught to use the hospital as a resort; neither do they have to experience long periods of hospitalization before they convert the hospital milieu into their "old hunting grounds." Instead, we find that first admissions enter the hospital with desires for a hedonic existence and within three weeks after admission are in fact living such a life.

It would seem difficult, for at least two reasons, to attempt to incorporate these findings into the dominant psychiatric paradigm of the schizophrenic. First, on an empirical basis we find that psychopathology as measured by diagnostic categories and Phillips scale scores does not correlate with any of our measures, including styles of hospital and community adaptation. Second, we find no differences between schizophrenics and nonschizophrenics on measures of hospital and community life or patient attitudes. Empirically, then, there is no evidence to suggest that pathology is at all relevant to the phenomenon under investigation. Indeed, the evidence of continuity of adaptation styles, their congruency with patient attitudes and goals, and their nonrelevance to the formal purposes of the hospital suggest quite directly the effectiveness of the patients and the ineffectiveness of the hospital as a force of intervention in the patients' lives. Neither of the commonly held assumptions that patients are ineffectual because of their pathology (for example, Redlich and Freedman, 1966) or because of debilitating and massive institutional pressures (for example, Goffman, 1961; Stanton and Schwartz, 1954) is supported by these data.

In summary, it appears that a substantial majority of open-ward patients in the hospital, those that have just arrived as well as those that have been there for some time, recognize the potential resort characteristics of the hospital; and when they are afforded the opportunity they actively and effectively subvert the institutional system in order to realize these potentials.

We believe that this victory does not go unsung; rather we would expect that ex-patients communicate their accomplishments to friends and acquaintances. Specifically, we assume that ex-patients tell their friends about the "good deal" that can be found in the mental hospital. As a consequence of these communications, one can predict that an accurate and extensive knowledge of the hedonic aspects of the hospital becomes established in neighborhoods that have a relatively large number of former patients. If these assumptions are correct, at least two further consequences can be anticipated. First, people who are friends of ex-patients should develop a more hedonistic orientation toward the hospital than people who do not have ex-patient friends. Second, hospitalization should appear to friends of ex-patients as a distinctly palatable event and in some instances even facilitate behavior that would lead to institutionalization. In order to test these assumptions two further studies were undertaken.

THE EFFECTS OF BEING FRIENDS WITH EX-PATIENTS ON ATTITUDES TOWARD THE HOSPITAL

This first study (B. Braginsky, D. Braginsky, K. Ring, and J. Holzberg) was concerned with the influence we assumed ex-patients have on their friends' attitudes about the hospital. We predicted that first-admission patients who have ex-patient friends would have attitudes upon entry to the hospital more similar to experienced patients (Old-timers) in the hospital than first-admission patients who do not have ex-patient friends.

METHOD

Eighty first-admission subjects (40 who had ex-patient friends and 40 who did not) were randomly selected for analysis. Both male and female subjects were equally distributed in each of the groups. Percentage agreement scores (scale positions of 4, 5, and 6) were then computed for each of the 86 PAT items for both groups of subjects. These agreement scores were then compared with the percentage of agreement scores of 189 experienced and long-term patients.

RESULTS AND DISCUSSION

The comparisons are presented in Table 22. As one can notice, first-admission patients are a homogeneous group. Item percentages do vary, however, between both groups of first admissions, and, if we compare the direction of each item deviation from the 189 Old-timers, the following results are obtained: (1) first-admission groups differ from each other on 73 items and (2), in comparing the direction of these differences, we find that first admission subjects with ex-patient friends are closer in percentage agreement with Old-timers on 57 of the 73 items (sign test yields an h of 25, $p < .001$). First-admission patients who have ex-patient friends have a profile significantly more similar to Old-timers in the hospital than first-admission patients with no ex-patient friends.

TABLE 22

Percentage Agreement on the 86 PAT Items

	OLD-TIMERS	FIRST ADMISSIONS WITH EX-PATIENT FRIENDS	FIRST ADMISSIONS WITH NO EX-PATIENT FRIENDS
1. More tax money should be spent in the care and treatment of people with severe mental illness.	89	97.5	97.5
2. Anyone who tries hard to better himself deserves the respect of others.	95	97.5	97.5
3. If our hospitals had enough well-trained doctors, nurses, and aides, many of the patients would get well enough to live outside the hospital.	96	95	95
4. A patient would be foolish not to try to enjoy himself as long as he is in the hospital.	84	90	72.5
5. In many ways a hospital is just like any other neighborhood you find on the outside.	71	55	40
6. It is important not to think about the life you lead outside the hospital as long as you are a patient.	48	40	35
7. The administrators of mental hospitals should make a strong effort to hire staff members who are able to get along with people.	95	100	97.5

TABLE 22 (continued)

	OLD-TIMERS	FIRST ADMISSIONS WITH EX-PATIENT FRIENDS	FIRST ADMISSIONS WITH NO EX-PATIENT FRIENDS
8. More than anything else, mental patients need the respect and understanding of the staff who work with them.	95	97.5	97.5
9. The best doctors and drugs cannot cure a mental patient unless the patient does everything he can do to help himself.	97	95	92.5
10. The best way to fit into hospital life is to try to have a good time.	79	77.5	70
11. If you really want to, it is not too hard to stay or leave the hospital.	71	70	72.5
12. It's possible to have a good and full life while you are a patient.	75	62.5	52.5
13. Although patients discharged from mental hospitals may seem all right, they should not be allowed to marry.	23	5	5
14. The best way to handle mental patients in mental hospitals is to keep them behind locked doors.	18	7.5	17.5
15. Regardless of how you look at it, patients with severe mental illness are no longer really human.	22	7.5	10
16. Once a mental patient, always a mental patient.	23	5	2.5
17. It's important for a mental patient to have a sense of humor.	89	87.5	85
18. There is nothing wrong with being a mental patient.	88	77.5	57.5
19. There is little that can be done for mental patients in a mental hospital except to see that they are comfortable and well fed.	40	10	15

TABLE 22 (continued)

	OLD-TIMERS	FIRST ADMISSIONS WITH EX-PATIENT FRIENDS	FIRST ADMISSIONS WITH NO EX-PATIENT FRIENDS
20. All patients in mental hospitals should be prevented from having children by a painless operation.	25	12.5	20
21. An employer would be foolish to hire a person who has been a patient in a mental hospital, even if he seems fully recovered and is well trained for the job.	23	7.5	7.5
22. There are many people on the outside more disturbed than a lot of Old-timers in the hospital.	84	95	72.5
23. It is good therapy to spend most of your time relaxing and enjoying your stay in the hospital.	75	72.5	67.5
24. Medication is more helpful to an individual than individual or group therapy.	55	32.5	30
25. It is a good thing to treat mental patients with kindness, but it will probably not do much toward helping them get well.	27	27.5	30
26. It would be hard to develop a close friendship with a person who has been a patient in a mental hospital.	34	10	10
27. People who were once patients in mental hospital are no more dangerous than the average citizen.	78	72.5	57.5
28. A patient should try to make his life as simple as possible while in the hospital.	80	80	60
29. Mental patients should spend time getting to know more about themselves by sitting down alone and thinking.	57	47.5	37.5

TABLE 22 (continued)

	OLD-TIMERS	FIRST ADMISSIONS WITH EX-PATIENT FRIENDS	FIRST ADMISSIONS WITH NO EX-PATIENT FRIENDS
30. If you want to, it is kind of easy to feel that you are not a patient in a mental hospital.	76	60	42.5
31. Most mental patients are willing to work.	76	75	57.5
32. If the children of mentally ill patients were raised by normal parents, they would probably not become mentally ill.	37	40	32.5
33. The patients in mental hospitals should have something to say about the way the hospital is run.	82	75	57.5
34. You have to get to know your doctor if you want to get out of the hospital.	74	65	50
35. The best way to get help for your mental problems is to keep busy and forget you are a patient.	76	65	72.5
36. Patients in a mental hospital should have as much freedom as they want.	76	60	30
37. It is possible to become mentally ill by believing very strongly that you are likely to suffer eternal punishment and torture after death.	58	65	67.5
38. There is little use in writing to public officials because they are not really interested in the problems of the average man.	46	45	37.5
39. Even if a person who has been a patient in a mental hospital seems fully recovered, he should not be given a driver's license.	24	12.5	5

TABLE 22 (continued)

	OLD-TIMERS	FIRST ADMISSIONS WITH EX-PATIENT FRIENDS	FIRST ADMISSIONS WITH NO EX-PATIENT FRIENDS
40. It is important to learn all about the hospital if you want to get things done and enjoy yourself.	85	77.5	80
41. I don't think there should be mental hospitals but only out-patient clinics.	27	15	17.5
42. Sometimes an aid can be more important in making your stay in the hospital more comfortable than a doctor.	74	82.5	87.5
43. Success is more dependent on luck than on real ability.	36	17.5	15
44. Many patients are capable of skilled labor even though in some ways they are very disturbed.	85	97.5	92.5
45. When a person has a problem or a worry, it is best not to think about it but to keep busy with pleasant things.	74	60	60
46. People with mental illness should never be treated in the same hospital as people with physical illness.	61	62.5	52.5
47. There is no excuse for not being in therapy.	71	72.5	67.5
48. The only hope for a patient is to get understanding.	80	82.5	52.5
49. A woman would be foolish to marry a man who has a severe mental illness, even though he seems fully recovered.	31	32.5	27.5
50. Anyone who is in a hospital for mental illness should not be allowed to vote.	28	20	20
51. Every mental hospital should be surrounded by a high fence and guards.	22	2.5	10

TABLE 22 (continued)

	OLD-TIMERS	FIRST ADMISSIONS WITH EX-PATIENT FRIENDS	FIRST ADMISSIONS WITH NO EX-PATIENT FRIENDS
52. The law should allow a woman to divorce her husband as soon as he has geen confined in a mental hospital with severe mental illness.	23	10	10
53. All most patients need is a period of relaxation to get on their feet again.	71	65	57.5
54. A patient should not think about leaving but rather how he can get well again.	84	85	97.5
55. A person who has been a patient in a mental hospital should not be allowed by law to hold high political office.	42	25	25
56. The main purpose of a mental hospital should be to protect the public from a mentally ill person.	52	30	30
57. Many people in our society are lonely and unrelated to their fellow human beings.	73	82.5	90
58. Everyone should have someone in his life whose happiness means as much to him as his own.	95	90	95
59. If you want to get well again, it is important to establish a comfortable routine in the hospital.	92	90	95
60. Mental patients should avoid hospital jobs because it makes it easier to want to stay in the hospital.	32	25	22.5
61. Patients should have more say as to whether they should leave or stay in the hospital.	76	62.5	45
62. One of the best spots in the hospital is the canteen.	78	65	55

TABLE 22 (continued)

	OLD-TIMERS	FIRST ADMISSIONS WITH EX-PATIENT FRIENDS	FIRST ADMISSIONS WITH NO EX-PATIENT FRIENDS
63. As a patient, one shouldn't spend time developing a social life in the hospital with other patients, especially if the other patients live in other buildings in the hospital.	42	42.5	37.5
64. I know of patients who are really well enough to leave, but they enjoy it here and want to stay.	79	70	50
65. If I am discharged, I will try to hide the fact that I was a patient in a mental hospital when I meet new people on the outside.	52	32.5	25
66. A patient should get to know the staff of the hospital before he starts to get treated for his condition.	65	47.5	57.5
67. The best way to learn about the hospital is to ask patients who have been there for some time.	63	57.5	37.5
68. A patient should never leave the hospital until he is completely cured.	78	77.5	62.5
69. A patient cannot get well unless he is prepared to suffer from his illness.	30	40	42.5
70. A hospital should not ask a patient to do what he has not done on the outside.	73	50	45
71. Patients will feel better if the hospital does not make any demands.	73	57.5	40
72. You should try to be on friendly terms with the staff on the ward.	97	97.5	95

TABLE 22 (continued)

	OLD-TIMERS	FIRST ADMISSIONS WITH EX-PATIENT FRIENDS	FIRST ADMISSIONS WITH NO EX-PATIENT FRIENDS
73. Everything a person does in the hospital, including having coffee in the canteen, is therapeutic.	78	80	70
74. Patients should be required to work at a job while they are in the hospital.	69	67.5	67.5
75. It would be good for patients if the hospital scheduled all their time in the hospital.	30	27.5	30
76. Most patients in a state hospital are not mentally ill.	58	48	45
77. Patients would get better if the staff did not bother them.	30	20	15
78. Everybody has a little bit of mental illness in him.	80	82.5	77.5
79. Patients should be permitted to go into town whenever they wish to.	70	22.5	20
80. A patient should try to meet as many other patients as possible rather than limiting himself to patients on his own ward.	81	80	80
81. It is better not to make friends with patients while you are in the hospital.	32	20	22.5
82. You should always do what the staff wants you to, even if you disagree with them.	75	70	57.5
83. Watching television is good therapy for a patient.	83	82.5	85
84. Patients should go to dances because it is a good way to socialize.	87	87.5	90

TABLE 22 (continued)

	OLD-TIMERS	FIRST ADMISSIONS WITH EX-PATIENT FRIENDS	FIRST ADMISSIONS WITH NO EX-PATIENT FRIENDS
85. It is often better not to have visitors from home because they may upset you.	28	25	20
86. Patients always come into the hospital because they are forced to by others.	43	15	17.5

These findings are consistent with the assumption that ex-patients communicate the "good deal" they had in the hospital and that the communication increases their audience's hedonic orientation toward patienthood and hospitalization. An alternative explanation, however, may be offered. It may, of course, be that ex-patients and their friends have the same attitudes toward the hospital and that this similarity existed prior to any specific communications about the hospital. Although we have no direct evidence to refute this interpretation, we do know that ex-patients and their friends discuss the hospital (see page 134), and, even if these discussions do not lead to a greater similarity of hedonistic attitudes they surely must reinforce or give support to the hedonistic orientations already held by each party.

Of course, it is quite conceivable that ex-patients recognize the wisdom behind the adage "action speaks louder than words" and thus go a step further in their attempts at convincing their friends about the "good deal" in the hospital. It might be, for example, that some ex-patients go so far as to invite their friends to join them for a stay in the hospital. In this manner the former patient accomplishes at least two goals. First, he maximizes his chances of leading his friend into the ranks of the leisure class, and, second, he can accomplish this while at the same time enjoying the hospital experience. These assumptions led us to the following study.

A STUDY OF FRIENDSHIP PATTERNS AMONG ADMISSIONS TO THE MENTAL HOSPITAL

If ex-patients (or at least a proportion of them) decided to engage in this somewhat dramatic adventure (that is, the subversion of the gatekeeping functions of the hospital), we would expect the following kinds of information to be disclosed by the study of admission records (B. Braginsky, D. Braginsky, K. Ring, and H. Arbor): a significant proportion of admissions to the hospital should (1) live close to each other in the community, that is, in the same or adjoining buildings, (2) be of the same sex and approximate age, (3) enter the hospital together, (4) be given the same diagnosis upon entry to the hospital, and (5) be paired in such a manner that one admission is an ex-patient while the other is a first admission. If these correspondences are revealed, we shall have indirect support for our assumption of prosletyzing among patients and patients-to-be.

METHOD

The total number of admissions from a single city for an 18-month period was studied. The choice of this city was based on the characteristics that (1) it was relatively large, (2) the hospital was located within its limits, and (3) admissions from this city were assigned to the most elegant unit in the hospital and in addition were guaranteed placement on the same wards.

A list of names and addresses of all admissions was compiled. With this list, addresses of admissions were located and plotted on a map of the city. In addition, the age, sex, admitting diagnosis, number of hospitalizations, and the date of admission of each subject were recorded.

RESULTS

There were 112 admissions during the 18-month period. It is noteworthy that not one admission occurred during the month of July and that only one person was admitted in August. When admission addresses were plotted on the city map, distinct clusters appeared. These clusters ranged in size from dyads, that is, two admissions who lived close to each other in the community, to a cluster composed of eight admissions. In total, 63 patients, or 56 percent of the admissions, formed various clusters in the community. Each cluster was composed of admissions who lived no further than 600 feet from each other, with the majority of admissions within each cluster living within 300 feet of each other. Fourteen of the clusters were composed of dyads, while eight clusters contained three or more members.

The first question we addressed was whether admissions who lived in close proximity in the community (that is, members of clusters) entered the hospital close in time. Table 23 presents the actual and chance distributions of time intervals between admissions to the hospital. In this analysis, clusters of more than two members were treated as dyads; thus in a three-member cluster the differences in time of admission was computed between all possible pairs, namely, A and B, A and C, and B and C. A perusal of the table shows that 69 percent of the members of clusters enter the hospital within four months of each other. By chance we would expect only 44 percent of the members to do so. This difference is significant ($x^2 = 11.40$, $p < .01$). In addition, another analysis was made in order to more adequately meet the assumption of independence. For this analysis, admissions from clusters containing an odd number of members were randomly excluded from analysis in order to obtain an even number of cluster members. Then within each cluster, random dyads were created; thus a five-member cluster was made into a four-member cluster and then two dyads were randomly created. The results obtained from this analysis also demonstrated that people who live close to each other in the community and who become admissions to a mental hospital enter the hospital significantly close in time.

SEX COMPOSITION OF CLUSTERS   Are clusters composed of more like-sex people than one would expect by chance? Because there is an equal number of male and female members of clusters, by chance each cluster should be composed of approximately equal numbers of men and women. If, however, friendship patterns define clusters, then each cluster should tend to be composed of like-sex members. Examining the distribution of men and women in each cluster, we find that 80 percent of them come from

TABLE 23

Actual and Chance Distributions of Time Intervals between Admissions to the Hospital

INTERVAL BETWEEN ADMISSION (MONTHS)	ACTUAL PERCENTAGE OF ADMISSIONS	CHANCE PERCENTAGE OF ADMISSIONS
0	.093	.055
1	.186	.104
2	.151	.098
3	.104	.092
4	.151	.086
5	.093	.080
6	.069	.074
7	.058	.068
8	.034	.062
9	.034	.056
10	.011	.050
11	.011	.044
12	.000	.038
13	.000	.032
14	.000	.026
15	.000	.020
16	.000	.014
17	.000	.008

like-sex clusters. Dyads are typically composed of either two men or two women; triads of either three men or three women. Thus 44 of the 63 admissions are matched with like-sex partners ($x^2 = 9.92, p < .01$).

AGE COMPOSITION OF CLUSTERS   Eighty-nine percent of the admissions deviate less than ten years from the mean age of their particular clusters. A random assignment of ages (using the same age data) offered only 51 percent of the cases deviating less than ten years. This difference is significant ($x^2 = 13.50$, $p < .01$). Homogeneity of age is thus another significant characteristic of clusters.

DIAGNOSTIC COMPOSITION OF CLUSTERS   In order to examine the similarity of admitting diagnosis among members of clusters, diagnostic categories were reduced to (1) schizophrenic, (2) psychotic but not schizophrenic, and (3) nonpsychotic. The schizophrenic and nonpsychotic categories accounted for 92 percent of the diagnoses. Within the larger clusters approximately 50 percent of their members were diagnosed as schizophrenic and the remaining 50 percent as nonpsychotic. The results, then, were not significant for clusters larger than two people. For dyads, however, a highly significant similarity was found. Twelve of the 14 dyads were composed of members who had identical diagnoses ($x^2 = 7.14$, $p < .01$). That is, dyads were either composed of two schizophrenics or two nonpsychotics.

EXPERIENCE COMPOSITION OF CLUSTERS   Twelve of the 14 dyads were composed of one member who was a readmission while the other was a first admission. Of the larger clusters, seven out of eight were composed of at least one first admission and one readmission member. Exposure to experienced patients is thus intriguingly high in clusters.

DISCUSSION

Residents of clusters have been seen to share a number of attributes. In order to corroborate our assumptions that this similarity of attributes reflects friendship patterns and ex-patient influence on admission rates, we interviewed all new admissions to the hospital unit where members of clusters are sent. Of the 30 new admissions in the unit, 18, or 60 percent of them, admitted having met in the hospital old acquaintances and friends that lived close to them in the community, a finding that supports the implications of the study of admission records.

If we couple the results of this chapter with those presented earlier, it appears more than plausible to assume that a relatively large portion of admissions to the hospital are indeed friends and enter the hospital together, not because they simultaneously "caught" schizophrenia but simply because they wanted to enjoy together the resort potentials of the mental hospital. Entrance to the hospital, therefore, does not necessarily reflect deficiency, helplessness, or societal rejection; rather, it may be seen as one form of patient control over the gatekeeping functions of the hospital.

These results emphasize the permeability of the hospital's boundaries.[32] The ability of patients to pass through the hospital's gates (in either direction) and their successful transplantation in the hospital of hedonic community life styles highlights the fluidity of the institution's boundaries. The hospital, then, no longer appears as a system that can effectively control the selection of members it wants to service nor can it act as an effective force of intervention in the life of its residents. Rather, a more humble portrayal is in order; the institution appears to be simply another place for people to visit or settle in. This is ironic indeed, for the mental health professionals have only recently attempted to integrate the hospital into community life; the mental patient, however, for some time now has already succeeded in doing just that.

Before we proceed to Chapter 5 some words of caution are in order. We do not mean to imply that mental patients, without a care in the world, are holding hands and frolicking merrily across the hospital grounds. This is neither typical behavior at resorts nor is it typical at the mental hospital. The findings suggest, rather, that a close parallel exists between the mental hospital and the resort, but that merriment is not a salient dimension. The similarities between these seemingly disparate social settings, instead, take the following forms: both social settings impose minimal external demands; offer their residents similar physical settings with corresponding social activities (such as swimming pools, movie theaters, lounges, and so on); do not expect their residents to be productive; maximize the residents' opportunity for choosing their desired life style; are explicitly service installations designed to refresh

---

[32]Mental patients are not the only persons who subvert the gatekeeping functions of the mental hospital. For example, Goffman (1961) has described the "betrayal funnel" in which the family and physicians collude to have people hospitalized when it is not necessarily indicated.

and refurbish their residents so that they are in a more advantageous position to meet life's demands on the outside.

Thus, the prime function of both facilities is not to produce merriment but to reduce stress and tension and to enhance comfort. The mental hospital in fact can be more successful in increasing individual comfort than the resort. Clearly, the resorts offer more elegant services than the mental hospital, but the hospital services are more greatly appreciated by their residents. For example, many residents at a mental hospital are relieved when they do not have to worry where their next meal will come from, how they will keep warm in the winter, or where they will sleep. Residents at resorts, however, generally lack this appreciation of meals, beds, baths, and other necessities of life.

The Mental Patient Reconsidered: An Assessment of Paradigms

We have now completed the presentation of our findings. Altogether nine separate studies utilizing the gamut of investigative techniques available to the social psychologist—experiment, questionnaire, attitude measurement, interview, observation, ecological analysis—have furnished evidence bearing on the mental patient and his way of life. In this chapter, by considering the paradigmatic implications of these findings, we return to many of the issues raised originally in Chapter 1. Let us see, first of all, what picture of the mental patient emerges when we review the principal findings from the studies described in the last three chapters.

We began by demonstrating that mental patients are apparently motivated to ingratiate themselves with the staff in a situation in which there is a vague threat to their self-interest if they were to do otherwise. Next, we showed that through the tactic of impression management, motivationally comparable patients give utterly contradictory self-descriptions, depending on what consequences for discharge they believe their answers will have. It will be recalled, for example, that chronic patients admit (or deny) symptoms when doing so presumably conveys an impression of being "mentally ill," whereas Newcomers attempt to foster precisely the opposite impression. It was this experiment that first suggested that many patients may prefer to remain in the hospital and will act in such a way as to justify their status as "mentally ill" individuals. Finally, the last experiment reported in Chapter 2 revealed that chronic schizophrenics can present themselves in a staff-patient interview setting so that they appear "sick" enough to deserve to remain in the hospital but not that "sick" that reassignment to a closed ward seems indicated. Clear evidence of these patients' interpersonal effectiveness in acting to satisfy their putative primary motivations was provided by the ratings of three psychiatrists.

Chapter 3 was concerned with the extent to which the manipulative abilities displayed by patients in the foregoing experiments actually served to permit them to exercise control over their own hospital fate. An initial exploratory study suggested very strongly that what patients learn about the hospital as well as how long they reside in it is determined to a much greater extent by patients' motivations and attitudes than by their psychopathological status or by institutional demands. A second study documented more directly the assertion that the way patients adapt to the hospital is in large measure a voluntary matter and clearly reflects an active and successful attempt to structure their everyday hospital routines to permit gratification of their dominant motivations and interests. Far from a massively controlling agency, the mental hospital under study here appeared if not to encourage then at least to condone several quite distinct styles of adaptation, with the consequence that patients are able to pursue almost untrammeled their own preferred way of life for virtually however long they may wish. In a third study it was possible to show that patients can enhance their chances of autonomy and its attendant benefits by selectively avoiding those members of the staff who, if they so chose, could limit patients' freedom. By making himself "invisible," as it were, a patient can minimize the threats to his style of life—and there is ample evidence to indicate that the pa-

tients who stand to profit most from this tactic are most likely to
exploit it.

Throughout Chapter 3 certain pervasive themes were apparent, some of which had been hinted at by the data of the preceding chapter. Here we find increasing support for the contentions
that many patients are indeed motivated to remain in, rather than
to leave, the hospital and that *they*—rather than the hospital staff
—effectively determine the discharge decision. And while they
reside in the hospital the patients themselves seem to be the principal architects of their own fate; the hospital functions merely
and mainly as a passive setting in which patients go about the
business of establishing their own kind of community. A recur-
rent motif in this chapter is that the hospital is really like a
playground or, perhaps more aptly, a resort where patients can,
with a minimum of staff detection or intervention, indulge their
hedonistic inclinations.

These themes, although occasionally underlined in the inter-
pretive portions of Chapter 3, are given their fullest expression in
the last chapter. Here we are afforded a glimpse into the mental
hospital that reveals both its recreational climate as well as its
continuities with patients' outside communities. What we discover
in this chapter is that how a patient was accustomed to spending
his leisure time *before* coming to the hospital is the best single
predictor of how he will live in the hospital; we find that many
patients come into the hospital with attitudes already very similar to the predominantly hedonistically inclined chronic patients
but that new patients with old friends who have already been in
the hospital are more similar still; we learn that many new admissions had lived suspiciously close to previously hospitalized
patients and that, in addition to being more similar on a number
of demographic variables than one would expect by chance, both
new and previously admitted patients coming from the same
neighborhood tend to enter the hospital at points too close in
time to be coincidental; we learn that virtually no one seeks admission during the warm summer months but that the demand
starts to rise when the weather begins to grow less pleasant; and
so on.

Now, plainly, certain inferences are difficult to resist; we shall
confine ourselves to two of them. First, patients communicate to
other prospective patients information concerning the kind of life

available at the hospital; this information makes the hospital appear sufficiently attractive to some persons that they eventually *decide* to become residents, and they do. The second inference is predicated on the validity of the description of hospital life given by experienced patients to potential ones: The hospital does permit a person to pursue the leisure time activities (sometimes even under the guise of treatment) that are only periodically available on the outside, leading one of our favorite patients to dub his institution "Sun Valley Hospital."

SOME PARADIGMATIC IMPLICATIONS

In this book we have tried to draw a portrait of the schizophrenic patient by describing how he lives in the hospital and by tracing the continuities between his ways of life inside and outside the hospital. The patient emerges as an individual who, for reasons we shall try to specify shortly, very often chooses, though not necessarily consciously, institutionalization as either an intermittent or enduring way of life. Once in the institution, the schizophrenic exploits his environment in a wholly effective and rational manner in order to extract from it personally satisfying outcomes. We may find it peculiar that some persons would select such a milieu in the first place, but what they do once inside is no more ineffectual or irrational than the activities of any other community of persons. It is extraordinary how predictable (and sensible!) the conduct of patients becomes once one assumes that, for the most part, they want to remain in the hospital and that they know what they are about! Structurally, their behavior may appear to be bizarre; analytically, it is easily derivable from the general principles of psychology.

A man is as he lives. And this platitudinous maxim goes to the heart of the deficiency in the psychiatric paradigm. To paraphrase Haley (1965), psychiatrists (and many clinical psychologists, too) have a trained incapacity to examine contexts. Ordinarily, they do not take the trouble to study the schizophrenic in his everyday environment (by now it is evident that the schizophrenic indirectly abets the psychiatrist's ignorance by the tactic of selective avoidance). If they did, they would eventually be forced to see—as we were forced to see—that their conception of the schizophrenic was seriously in error and would necessarily remain so until they began to observe his behavior in less restricted settings than their own private offices. There, all sorts of fantasies about the patient's "psychic structure and functioning" may be safely entertained without risk that they will in any way be challenged by the concrete realities of the patient's actual situation. Inferences founded on such a narrow data-base must ultimately be rooted primarily in a kind of psychiatric mythology about the "nature" of schizophrenics instead of stemming, as they should, from the *behavior* of schizophrenics. Surely the spinning-out of gossamer-like theories that come apart with their first exposure to the stiff winds of the schizophrenic's everyday world is not a justifiable enterprise for intelligent and otherwise perspicacious men! These theories can thrive only in an encapsulated environment; schizophrenics, unfortunately, live elsewhere.

In denying the validity of the psychiatric paradigm, we need to make explicit just what it is that we are urging to be discarded. First of all, in our view, the problem of schizophrenia is not a medical problem, and its "treatment" is therefore a matter concerning which doctors do not have any special competence. We agree with Szasz (1961) that it is misleading and indeed dangerous to regard schizophrenia as some sort of "disease" for which the remedy is some manner of "cure." Such a position bestows custody of the schizophrenic to the medical profession merely on the basis of an unfortunate analogy—a state of affairs whose inappropriateness can be most eloquently affirmed only by those who have been its victims. In our opinion, the problem of schizophrenia is one that grows out of the patient's relationships with others as well as out of his relationship with society as a whole. It is remarkable how so many students of schizophrenia will agree with this now perfectly banal proposition and still be blind to its implications for the psychiatric paradigm. Later in this chapter we shall be more specific concerning how we conceive the problem of schizophrenia.

Second, we now formally propose that the term schizophrenia (and its various subclassifications) be dropped altogether from our scientific discourse and that all correlative expressions, tainted by the psychiatric perspective, such as *mental hospital* and *mental patient*, be abandoned also. No justifiable purpose is served by retaining such terms, however handy, if, by doing so, they obscure or falsify reality.

R. D. Laing, the British existentialist psychiatrist, in a somewhat similar context, recently (1967) confessed that "I do not myself believe that there is any such 'condition' as 'schizophrenia.'" Neither do we. It is a term without an ostensive referent, and, lacking any, it cannot even be said to have outlived its usefulness, because there is no reason to think that it ever had any. Accordingly, the sooner we are rid of it, the better.

Now we are of course aware that this proposal to scrap the construct of schizophrenia will make many people acutely uncomfortable despite the fact that others before us have advocated doing so (see Szasz, 1961, for example), especially because we have not suggested any term by which to replace it.[33] Still, there are obviously precedents in other sciences that have not only withstood the loss of a concept previously regarded as indispensable but that actually underwent an astonishing period of revitalization as a consequence. To have had to contemplate a chemistry without phlogiston or a physics without ether must initially have been a profoundly unsettling experience for those whose scientific world-view hinged on these concepts; yet subsequent generations of chemists and physicists, far from regretting their demise, must have wondered how they could have retained their scientific respectability for so long when, in hindsight, they functioned mainly to cripple scientific understanding. Surely the venerability of a concept is only an obstacle, not an argument; and the fact that casting aside a concept cherished in use and sanctified by tradition will cause a kind of dread for many can only be viewed as one of the inevitable effects of a scientific revolution.

A successful revolution not only destroys but builds. Those who question or resist our revolutionary objectives can therefore legitimately challenge us with the following counterargument: "You ask us no longer to speak of schizophrenia—you say it does not exist. Very well. But what do you offer us instead? The people we are used to calling schizophrenics exist. Do you deny that they have symptoms or that they suffer? Do you think we should abandon them when we abandon the term *schizophrenia*? If schizo-

[33]We could hardly do that without falling into a logical snare, of course. If schizophrenia is a construct without a specifiable referent, as we have argued, to substitute another term to denote that nothing would only restore the original problem in a new verbal guise. Obviously, a part of the difficulty here is semantic, and we shall return to this question of substitutability later in the chapter.

phrenics are ultimately no different from the rest of us, then why do only they end up in institutions? You act as if the solution of the problem of schizophrenia depends only on accepting the decree that the condition does not exist, that it is entirely fabricated and perpetuated by psychiatrists. We do not dispute your data nor do we negate your conclusion that under certain conditions schizophrenics can act in a reasonably normal and goal-directed fashion. What we do question is whether your point of view allows us to see any more clearly precisely what distinguishes the schizophrenic—or whatever you wish to call him—from others and which causes 'him to come to our attention in the first place."

The issues raised in this counterargument are of crucial importance in explicating and defending our position; it is therefore imperative that we deal with them directly.

The cardinal argument in our rebuttal is predicated on Kuhn's assertion, mentioned in Chapter 1, that a scientific revolution always entails one paradigm's being substituted for another. The problem with which the overthrown paradigm attempted to deal does not therefore disappear when another paradigm triumphs; it is simply conceived of in a new way.

In the present case, we do not assert that the problem for which the psychiatric paradigm offered an explanation was in any sense a false or meaningless problem; we assert only that it was misconstrued. Of course, individuals who were (and still are) labeled as schizophrenic are individuals who have difficulties in living; so do we all. Our position implies, however, that the nature of these difficulties is not clarified by alluding to "symptoms" or to other concepts based on a medical model. Our common task is to understand the behavior of individuals. We submit that the set of assumptions underlying the psychiatric paradigm that have been used to understand the behavior of institutionalized individuals have been either shockingly beside the point or erroneous and plainly, in our judgment at least, do not warrant being retained.

What can substitute for them? What, finally, is the shape of the new paradigm? Let us admit that it is not enough either to deny that the institutionalized individual is diseased or to affirm his humanity. We are still left with the hard question why he should come to reside in an institution while the rest of us remain outside. Indeed, we believe that the question must be formulated in this manner because only by doing so can one begin to see the outlines of an answer that would be consistent with the data presented in this book. Any new paradigm, we would argue, must not ignore these findings, even if they alone are not sufficient to confirm its validity. In the next section we shall offer an adumbration of such a paradigm. It represents a (necessary) *extension* of the already well supported alternative paradigm proposed in Chapter 1, and we present it, for once, with all the caution and tentativeness appropriate to its incomplete and fragile structure. We admit that we shall have to be uneasily speculative in much of what we say here. One of the functions of a new paradigm is to suggest how research questions ought to be framed, but because this now extended paradigm has not yet been tried out, we necessarily lack many of the answers we should like to have. If the paradigm has merit, however, these gaps will be bridged ultimately by empirical linkages, and one justification for sketching the paradigm here is that such gaps may thereby be more easily seen.

TOWARD A NEW PARADIGM: THE QUEST FOR ASYLUM

Every society provides its members with a number of alternative routes through life or careers. In simple societies, the range of choices may be restricted: farmer, warrior, or priest. In a technologically complex society such as ours, the number of such possibilities is legion. One possibility, not sanctioned by our society but made inevitable by it, is to withdraw altogether from it. One simply ceases to be a functioning, productive member of society. Why should this become a way of life for some?[34]

[34]In a general sense, there are two classes of reasons that may be distinguished. One may withdraw from society either because one is in intellectual disagreement with its prevailing values or demands or because one simply cannot cope with societal pressures. There would seem to be little doubt that both factors play a part in determining societal defections, although it seems equally clear that the relative weight and interaction of these factors is quite different for different categories of persons (for example, alienated college students versus alcoholics). In what follows, we emphasize the inability rather than the unwillingness to adjust to society's demands; we recognize, however, that both factors may often be intertwined in such a way that the distinction becomes difficult to defend.

The broad outlines of the answer are not difficult to make out. The dominant fact about our society today, as Keniston (1965), among many others, has pointed out, is virtually unregulated technological change. It is a society that is continually leaving us behind the times because the times never stand still. There can be few of us who do not occasionally feel the terror of living in a world over which we seemingly have no control. The sheer fact of ceaseless change—especially technological change—has immense consequences for our feelings of psychological well-being. Hoffer, in several of his essays (1963, 1967) has argued persuasively that every change brings a crisis in self-esteem; constant change means a continuous crisis. Men do not know whether they can cope with the most recent innovations; they are every day confronted with fresh evidence of their growing obsolescence; life becomes overly complex, it demands too much.

Little wonder, then, that Hoffer can write that drastic change creates a population of misfits. As the jetsam of a changing society, they have available only a single possibility: to find a way to live *outside* society. There could be fewer prospects more inviting to persons caught in such circumstances than to take up residence in a "mental institution."

Even before the days of such tremendously accelerated technological change, there were, of course, many who sought the shelter of institutional life. In nineteenth century New England, for example, although state mental hospitals as we know them today did not exist, there were institutions housing individuals whose social circumstances were decidedly similar to those of present-day mental patients. In reviewing the history of one such institution, Stearns and Ullman (1949) remind us that our contemporary "mental institutions" often had their beginnings as almshouses and, thus, originally served as refuges for the poor, the lame, and the infirm. The delineation of our paradigm can, in fact, be conveniently facilitated by examining the development of the state hospital at Tewksbury, Massachusetts (which is the institution Stearns and Ullman discuss) and the composition and background of its residents over the years.

In 1854, in response to an influx of Irish immigrants following the great famine of 1846, the state of Massachusetts constructed three almshouses for the "unsettled poor," one of which was located in Tewksbury. At first, the administration was completely in the hands of nonmedical personnel. The history of this institution, however, is one of gradual transformation into a medical facility. Stearns and Ullman write:

> . . . the last 94 years has seen the constant withdrawal from the unsettled poor classification into the medical classification. In 1869, despite the institution of public care for the insane, there was still a large component of such cases, and buildings were erected for these. . . . By 1883 the superintendent was a physician and since then the medical features have grown, until in 1900 the name was changed from State Almshouse to State Hospital; in 1909, from State Hospital to State Infirmary; and finally, in 1939, to Tewksbury State Hospital and Infirmary. Gradually caretakers were replaced by nurses and the supervision became medical (pp. 803–809).

Who are the people who are the recipients of this medical treatment? According to a survey taken in 1843, prior to the establishment of the almshouse at Tewksbury, the "insane" (by mid–nineteenth-century standards) constituted only a minority of 30 percent of the inmates of such public institutions. We are indebted to Stearns and Ullman for more relevant data; they took the trouble to examine the records for Tewksbury itself for the years 1854 to 1948. Although himself a psychiatrist, the senior author found that, in his analysis of Tewksbury's population, medical classification afforded "little insight as to the kind of persons we are dealing with." At the outset, of course, these persons were typically the "unsettled poor": immigrants, children, the jobless. Who are they today? On the basis of interviews with new admissions, Stearns and Ullman describe them as follows:

> The individuals show an excess of immigrants; a deficit in formal education, in occupational skill, and in marital success. We do not find a preponderance of catastrophic illness, but we do find alcohol to have been an important factor in the failure of these individuals to make a successful adaptation. . . . It is not possible to squeeze them into the categories of mental disease, however much elasticity we may be willing to use. Yet they have never functioned successfully in a competitive society. Their relatives and friends would have nothing to do with them; they have worn them out or shamed them to the point where they wished no further contact (p. 808).

It appears, then, that it is largely owing to indiscriminate psychiatric branding that the poor of the nineteenth century have been transformed into the mentally ill of the twentieth. What has changed is our system of classification; the social situation of the residents of our public institutions, such as mental hospitals, has remained remarkably constant. Our present-day "mental patients" are only the societal descendants of the nineteenth-century poor. At this point in history, they constitute one type in the category of socially rejected individuals—they are today's castoffs, the misfits of twentieth-century American life, rootless and unwanted.

This characterization of the "mental patient" as a social reject, as one who lacks ordinary stable social connectedness, does not stem simply from a desire to describe him so that he fits neatly into our paradigm. If one looks at how ex–mental patients live and are treated once they leave the hospital, we find the evidence that both corroborates our depiction of patients and makes us understand why institutional life should be so attractive to them.

In one large follow-up study of ex–mental patients in California (Miller, 1968), for example, it was found that within five years of discharge, 71 percent of the sample had returned to the hospital at least once and that nearly a quarter had returned an average of 4.4 times. About 85 percent of these ex-patients, according to Miller, "stemmed originally from the poorest class" and 65 percent never finished high school. After discharge, only about a quarter were able to work and a like number existed entirely on public welfare. In California, although 85 percent of all adults are married, only 48 percent of these released patients were. Miller reports that of these, the majority had "only marginal or casual connections with their families—they were not heads of houses, nor did they have important roles in family affairs, maintenance or support. In general they were on the fringes, dependent and 'extra', often unwelcome guests in other people's homes (p. 38)." "Generally," Miller concluded, "they were important to nobody!" Among those who were unmarried, a drifter's life seems to have been common. Of these, Miller comments:

> Many lived alone. Typically, these stayed in skid row hotels and were on relief. Some, though adult, moved back with parents—who were very frequently aged and infirm, barely able to take care of

themselves, subsisting mostly on state welfare and social security. Those who lived with relatives generally found themselves becoming cinderellas in other people's chimney corners (p. 38).

There is no reason to think that this characterization of the mode of life and level of social acceptance of ex–mental patients is markedly unrepresentative of those who have spent time in state institutions. And if it is at all accurate, then we can grasp— without having the slightest need to assume that such individuals must be "mentally ill"—what features of institutional life would be likely to induce a new or former "mental patient" to remain a voluntary resident. Suppose we now consider the rewards and costs of that alternative for persons for whom the price of continuing membership in society is already too high.

Institutional life, as reflected in the preceding pages of this book, obviously has many advantages. First of all, one moves into a world that will provide some sense of temporal stability; it is as if one steps out of a maddening swirling river onto the comforting, immobile shore. Second, it is a simpler world and one, as we have shown, over which it is possible to exercise a considerable amount of fate-determination. Third, leisure time activities, and, in general, a hedonistic pursuit of them, are not only possible but are embedded into the very structure of hospital life itself. Such an environment, we submit, would be appealing to *anyone,* but especially to a person for whom the outer world is a source chiefly of melancholy and despair.

What about the costs? There are minor restrictions on one's freedom, but no one who has read the last two chapters will be anxious to argue that most residents chafe a great deal under such restrictions; they are, most of them, too busy exploiting their freedom to notice that they do not have *absolute* freedom. A second cost is that incurred simply by acquiring the stigma of being a "mental patient." But inasmuch as (1) that is a matter of consequence mainly after one is released from the hospital and (2) many residents intend to either settle in for a protracted stay or return, like tourists, at periodic intervals, the stigmatizing effect of institutionalization does not appear to be so much of a disadvantage as it otherwise might be. There is, finally, the annoyance of having to convince the staff that one is mad, but because they are prepared to believe it almost no matter how one behaves, that is little more than a slight imposition.[35]

Weighing the reward-cost balance, it seems to us that to seek entrance into an institution and to desire to remain there scarcely justifies the conclusion that residents of "mental hospitals" are individuals whose sanity is no longer intact. Rather, the opposite conclusion seems called for: the residents who remain in "mental hospitals" are behaving in a perfectly rational manner to achieve a personally satisfying way of life—often the most satisfying of which they are capable. There is, then, nothing mysterious about why they go into the institution or why they stay.[36]

Some qualifications must now be entered in order to forestall misunderstanding.

First, we have argued that in a certain sense an individual *chooses* his career as a mental patient; it is not thrust upon him as a consequence of his somehow becoming "mentally ill." But in just what sense does the individual "choose" his career? In our view, having and maintaining the status of a mental patient is the outcome of *purposive* behavior. Furthermore, given the life circumstances of most of the persons who become and remain residents of mental hospitals, their doing so evinces a realistic appraisal of their available alternatives; it is, in short, a *rational* choice. To affirm that the individual is acting in a purposive and rational manner and that his eventual condition is in no way fortuitous does *not necessarily* imply that he is consciously calculating in his behavior. It is obvious that rational goal-directed behavior does not guarantee that the individual appreciates what he is up to. It is equally obvious that the residents described in

[35]We are being tongue-in-cheek here. Many residents suffer, and suffer intensely, from real problems and are not always merely putting on a convincing display for the staff. Very often, however, a resident's most pronounced difficulties coincide with his first few days of institutionalization and no doubt largely reflect the process of adaptation. In any case, we think that *all* of a resident's behavior can ultimately be encompassed within a nonpsychiatric paradigm.

[36]From this analysis it follows that persons who fail to pursue an institutional career, even though they would be labeled by psychiatrists as "schizophrenic," were they ever to be examined, do so for one of three reasons: (1) their reward-cost balance outside the hospital is sufficiently positive to keep them there; (2) they underestimate the rewards or overestimate the costs of hospital life, or both; or (3) they simply are unaware of institutionalism as a possible career.

this book frequently must have been consciously manipulative; many of our findings would be inexplicable without making such an assumption.[37] All we are claiming here is that it is not necessary to suppose that the choice to become a mental patient always reflects a state of conscious volition.

Second—and this should be apparent—the argument just developed is meant to apply mainly to the person who comes to be labeled "the chronic schizophrenic." It is he who makes up the bulk of the permanent inhabitants of mental hospitals and who has apparently proved most refractory to treatment procedures. To some extent, however, this analysis is appropriate to anyone who remains for some time in the institution. It is even applicable in principle to the Newcomers in the hospital who, it will be recalled from Chapter 2, were as a whole motivated to leave and who engaged in impression management to promote that objective. Here the motivations (and presumably the reward-cost balance) were different from those of the Old-timers, but the same *mode* of analysis (in terms of motivational factors and relative preference for hospital-available outcomes over those attainable in their outside communities) can easily be conducted. We would hope, in fact, that one of the more direct applications of the paradigm we are here proposing would consist of this kind of analysis for different classes of persons over a wide variety of institutional settings.

Finally, one may ask: because there are several ways of withdrawing from society, what determines whether the individual will choose the particular path of insitutionalization? That question is at the present utterly beyond our ability to answer. Here the most extensive and careful research is needed before we can hope to have even the beginnings of an answer. It is conceivable that much of the work already conducted into the etiology of schizophrenia could, if appropriately recast, be helpful in a quest for the relevant variables. We would caution, however, that it is naive to imagine the answers would lie exclusively in the sphere of familial structure. It seems to us that a more promising approach would be one modeled after Keniston's (1965) analysis of alienation in the college student. In searching for the roots of

[37]For a trenchant discussion of the difficulties of determining conscious intent in manipulative behavior, the reader is referred to Goffman (1959), Chapter 2.

this kind of alienation, Keniston disdained a simple causative model and argued instead that the condition could not be understood without reference to a network of interdependent factors including both the student's family constellation and the nature of modern American society. Our paradigm, too, suggests the wisdom of adopting an enlarged perspective if we are ever to understand why some people, but not others, leave society by withdrawing into institutional life.

PROSPECTS FOR THE NEW PARADIGM

In both the introductory and the present chapter we have indicated some reasons why there is resistance to *any* new paradigm. In the case of the paradigm we have advanced, there are in addition some special and powerful forces which will undoubtedly delay its acceptance or perhaps even prevent it altogether. Acceptance of the present paradigm obviously undercuts the *raison d'être* of the psychiatrist in the "mental hospital"; in our conception there is simply no need of him or any other ancillary personnel whose presence is now legitimized only by the assumed relevance of a medical model. To express matters in so blunt a fashion may seem harsh, but this paradigmatic implication is clearly inescapable however one chooses to phrase it. No one likes to be told of his dispensability, especially when such a judgment demands that one graciously surrender his considerable power; the reaction of the psychiatric community is therefore predictable. Society, too, has a stake in maintaining the psychiatric perspective. No society can tolerate the thought that those who choose to desert it may be acting in a rational manner. Society's deviants, like doctors' mistakes, have to be explained away, and the assumption that "the insane are not responsible for their actions" provides the proper and indeed the perfect explanation. Obviously, only someone who is quite mad (or "not in his right mind," "duped," "misguided") could commit such a treasonable act. Our paradigm of course suggests a different interpretation.

From this point of view the psychiatric paradigm may be seen to be the handmaiden of society's refusal to face some unpalatable truths about itself. By providing a reassuring interpretation of society's deviants, psychiatry not only justifies its own existence but also unwittingly insures the perpetuation of a scandalous double hypocrisy: "the myth of mental illness" continues to be foisted, enabling a complacent society to misconceive utterly the nature of its most essential reforms.

The prospects of endorsement of our paradigm within a short time plainly are not bright, for, as Kuhn observes: "the transfer of allegiance from paradigm to paradigm is a conversion experience that cannot be forced (p. 150)."

For the time being we—like all revolutionaries—must look toward the future and hope that the state of affairs depicted by Kuhn (1962) will ultimately describe the fate of our paradigm:

> At the start a new candidate for a paradigm may have few supporters, and on occasions the supporters' motives may be suspect. Nevertheless, if they are competent, they will improve it, explore its possibilities, and show what it would be like to belong to the community guided by it. And as that goes on, if the paradigm is one destined to win its fight, the number and strength of the persuasive arguments in its favor will increase. More scientists will then be converted, and the exploration of the new paradigm will go on. Gradually the number of experiments, instruments, articles, and books based upon the paradigm will multiply. Still more men, convinced of the new view's fruitfulness, will adopt the new mode of practicing normal science, until at last only a few elderly holdouts remain (p. 158).

The Cooperative Retreat: An Alternative to the Mental Hospital

Just as the quest to understand "mental illness" has plagued man, so too has he been searching for an answer to what to do with persons who act in a bizarre manner. When one examines from an historical perspective how the mentally ill have been treated, it becomes apparent that the treatment is intimately related to the paradigm of the time as well as to the prevailing social attitudes. In order to illustrate the paradigm-treatment parallels, a brief sketch will be presented below.

A HISTORICAL REVIEW OF THE TREATMENT OF THE "MENTALLY ILL"

Before the advent of modern psychiatry, and especially during the Middle Ages, persons exhibiting deviant behavior were thought to be possessed by the devil or his cohorts. The treatment, then, necessitated the driving out, either by prayer or torture, of these demons. Widespread and indiscriminate practice of exorcism eventually gave rise to the unbridled fanaticism seen in the witch hunts of the seventeenth century.

A revolt ensued whereby an attempt was made to find a more rational and humane paradigm. And so theologians replaced demon possession with the "wild beast" theory, where unorthodox behavior was considered a reversion to man's lower animal nature, and, therefore, must be beaten out of the person so that he might rise again to his human sensibilities. The medical profession, frowning upon this theological explanation, took a radical position, declaring that insanity was caused by a diseased brain. Because afflicted persons were thought to be insensitive and unaware of their surroundings, violent types of medical treatment were prescribed. Thus, the early forms of torture gave way to medicinal blood-letting and emetics.

At the close of the eighteenth century an enlightened public put an end to this oppressive treatment and stressed instead respect for the dignity of the individual, sane or insane. In keeping with the temper of the times, physicians adopted a paradigm of mental illness that de-emphasized organic aspects while emphasizing the functional nature of the disorder. Mental illness was seen as being induced by events and situations external to the individual; that is, it was the result of an individual's experiences. The treatment, therefore, involved placing the insane in a pleasant environment, immersed in brotherly love, so that their inner harmony and power of reason might be restored or, if necessary, developed. The key to "moral treatment" (as this system was called) was respect for the moral rights of the insane as people, treating them with kindness and sensitivity. The physician perceived his patients as members of a family of which he was the figurehead; his task, as well as that of the institution, was to help to advance the development of the patients as human beings.

Respect for the dignity of the individual underwent a massive change shortly after the Civil War in America, a change which was reflected in the standards of care and concern for the mentally ill. The medical paradigm of this period reverted to the disease hypotheses and assumed further that insanity was a degenerative illness afflicting only persons with inferior constitutional heredity. Using Darwin's theory as a basis, doctors saw mental illness as one of nature's ways of eliminating the unfit of the species. But because it was not in keeping with religious and philosophical principles to allow nature to take its course, the responsibility for the survival of the insane was assumed by society. Any hopes of rehabilitation were beyond the realm of possibility, and treatment, therefore, was out of the question—the only thing to be done with the insane was to put them away and lock them up. And so the benevolent doctor became no more than a keeper of inmates, and the institution became a prison rather than an asylum.

Although some exist even today, custodial institutions began to be replaced by therapeutic ones shortly after World War I. Contrary to our earlier examples, this revolution in the treatment of the mentally ill, the move toward the total therapeutic community, was not preceded by any discernable revolution in psychiatric conceptions. In fact, the implicit-belief system of the dominant psychiatric conception today, presented in Chapter 1, is strikingly similar to many earlier conceptions. At present, as in the past, for example, schizophrenics are viewed as something less than human; their illness is seen as a disintegrative disease process that, if not properly and promptly treated, may result in almost total psychic dysfunction. Moreover, it is still maintained that schizophrenics are the pawns of fate, unable to control their intrapsychic and external affairs, that they are people "in whom and to whom things happen."

The radical shift from custodial to therapeutic treatment, then, was not the outcome of a new paradigm but rather of a synthesis and elaboration of old ones different from the prevailing conception at the turn of the century.

But despite the multitude of innovative therapeutic techniques employed today, the ever increasing number of trained personnel, and all their good intentions and strenuous efforts, statistics show clearly that even in the most active and up-to-date therapy centers in the world, the number of persons who have been successfully "rehabilitated" is painfully small. The results are, in fact, no better than those obtained decades ago by "moral treatment" (Brockoven, 1963) and, as Eysenck (1966) points out, about the same as no treatment whatsoever. Even the "round-the-clock" milieu therapies, where the hospital is conceived as a "therapeutic community" (Jones, 1953), when subjected to the critical eye of research prove to be ineffective agents of change (see Fairweather, 1964).

The long history of repeated failures has caused some prominent psychiatrists to pause and reflect on this depressing state of affairs. But their analysis of this situation, which seems to be largely a defensive one, has resulted only in the condemnation of institutions, blaming the hospital for "creating" chronic mental patients rather than re-evaluating their own ideology and treatment programs. And so individual psychotherapy, group therapy, family therapy, occupational therapy, and all the other therapies have now moved into community mental health centers, where the hospital cannot interfere with their "curative powers."

We believe, however, that this also does not provide an adequate solution and will again lead to failure and disappointment. Even in the most ideal situation with the most ideal patient, it has never been demonstrated that these therapies are effective, much less with the kinds of people whom we have encountered in the mental hospital.

It may be recalled that the patients we studied entered the hospital, for the most part, in order to pursue an hedonic life in a comfortable, nondemanding milieu. They did not perceive themselves as being particularly ill or, for that matter, any different than people in general. In fact, while in the hospital a mere 10 percent got involved in some form of psychotherapy, and only because they had been assigned to it. Their average treatment period, not surprisingly, was only four weeks, and in no case did it exceed two months.

Just because community mental health centers have been established, there is no reason to suppose that they will be used by former or potential mental patients. On the contrary, the evidence seems to indicate that their goal is not to avoid hospitalization by seeking early "treatment." Moreover, the persons selected by the staff for treatment at these elegant centers are the applicants whose interests and goals are most compatible with the interests and goals of the staff (that is, educated, articulate, middle-class "believers"). The future of these centers, therefore, appears to be as dismal as psychiatry's earlier attempts to solve the problem of "mental illness."

A "SUCCESSFUL" ATTEMPT TO
REHABILITATE CHRONIC PATIENTS

Recently, social psychologists have begun to move in on the treatment turf, producing some surprising results. Fairweather and his associates (1964) developed an innovative treatment program aimed at getting chronic mental patients out into the community and working. By using small-group techniques, the patients' dependency on the hospital staff was discouraged, and the patients themselves were given the lion's share of the responsibility for making decisions concerning their own hospitalization. The minimizing of the staff's involvement in decision making and the concomitant increase in patient power led to a high rate of discharge among the chronic patients who participated in this program. A more recent study (Towbin, 1968) of a similar rehabilitation effort also yielded an impressive discharge rate for chronic patients as well as a low rate of recidivism (6 percent after six months). In both programs, prior to discharge, patients had to submit for approval by the staff a work-and-living plan. Thus, patients who had been living in the hospital for many years and who appeared refractory to numerous therapeutic attempts were able to find employment and a place of residence in the community.

In order to explicate the treatment implications of our model (which will be spelled out shortly) as well as to extricate them from these "social psychological" treatment programs, let us examine more closely the criteria of success and exactly what is meant by rehabilitation.

To take issue with the economic fact that it is cheaper for society when hospitalized patients leave to work in the community would be absurd. By the same token, most of us would agree that practical, economic considerations should not be used to evaluate the success of a treatment program. Psychiatrists, psychologists, and other mental health professionals are not the bankers and brokers of society's welfare funds.

What, then, justifies the notion that to live and work outside of the hospital are the criteria of successful rehabilitation? The moralistic and normative nature of these criteria are, we feel, pitifully obvious: to live in a mental hospital is a "bad" thing, whereas to be a gainfully employed resident of a community is a "good" thing. Rehabilitation, then, is not the remaking in an *improved* form, as the "rehabilitators" claim, but rather the making over in an *approved* form. The mental health professionals, in their attempts to re-educate, re-motivate, re-what-have-you, have become the agents of society, rewarding compliance and social desirability rather than somehow enhancing the individual in "treatment." The ethics of these practices and the basis upon which they are founded are, indeed, questionable.

TREATMENT IMPLICATIONS OF OUR MODEL

We have in Chapter 5 already proposed that the concepts of schizophrenia, mental illness, and other allied concepts be discarded and that mental hospitals be abandoned. Because our paradigm and research suggest that there is nothing radically different about mental patients, that they are like everyone else except that they do not quite "make it" (or do not want to keep "making it") in our complex society, the treatment implications are perhaps not immediately obvious. It is important, therefore, at this point, to dispel any misleading impressions or distortions of our position that may have been unintentially conveyed.

Our indictment of the current psychiatric paradigm and practices is in no way meant to imply that the people living in mental hospitals are "freeloaders" who should be cast out and forced back into society. This would certainly not be a solution to the problems that beset the ever increasing residue of people who simply cannot keep abreast with the changing times. Like most of us, these people do have problems in living, and they do become enmeshed in intolerable situations outside the hospital gates. Life in the hospital, therefore, represents a temporary refuge from society for some, while for others it constitutes a permanent withdrawal.

The paradigm we put forth suggests that, short of a transformation of society, the best solution would be to provide opportunities (other than mental hospitals) for withdrawal and *renewal;* opportunities that would eliminate the otherwise unavoidable hypocrisy of mental hospitals that require people to assume the degrading status of patienthood in order to obtain some relief from societal pressures.

Throughout history there have been isolated examples of societies as well as subgroups that tried to provide for their members dignified retreats from the mainstream of life. For example, in the Middle Ages, people who felt that life was too demanding could, with societal approval and respect, choose to live in a monastery (Robert Knapp, personal communication). Today these people would, no doubt, be subjected to at least a raised psychiatric eyebrow and, possibly, to degrading internment in a mental institution. Centuries later the Society of Friends, under the leadership of 'Tuke, provided a retreat, a house "situated a mile from York, in the midst of a fertile and smiling countryside," for the troubled and financially impoverished members of that group (see Foucault, 1965).

In our society, at present, there exists, for those who can afford it, a wide choice of temporary retreat facilities including those sponsored by religious organizations, spas and other health resorts, as well as the hunting lodge in the mountains and the cottage by the sea. Clearly, these facilities provide a much needed respite from everyday activities. Yet what alternatives are available "to get away from it all" for the less affluent members of our society? Where can they, without having to use the currency of self-respect and self-esteem, renew themselves?

Here, as in most civilized societies, the social welfare of the populace is a major concern. But, unlike most societies, our social assistance programs have many limiting conditions. That is, help should be given to all those who need it:

provided they can afford it
provided they can show that they cannot afford it without outside (i.e., government) help (i.e., the means test)
provided they are worthy of it ("the worthy poor")
provided they do not have a man living in the home
provided they are of correct lineage, color, religion, etc. (Vail, 1968, p. 13).

In sharp contrast to our qualified social help policy, for Scandinavians (see Vail, 1968) giving help to *all* those who need it is not merely a principle but a reality. Moreover, their definition of "need" is so encompassing as to include what we consider luxuries. For example, Sweden provides, at the expense of the state (here a means test is employed), vacations for mothers, recognizing and *responding* to the need of harassed mothers to get away from it all, even for a little while. The "mental health" implications of practices such as this are obvious.

We do not mean to imply that in this society human "needs" are not recognized but rather that we neglect or, perhaps, refuse to respond appropriately to them. This has been made all too clear by the recent reports concerning poverty and hunger in the midst of our vast wealth and resources. When social reforms and welfare programs are implemented they are usually in response not to the "needs" of the people but to the crises which have grown out of the too long ignored "needs."

We propose that in response to the vital needs of its members society make available a legitimate and dignified "out," instead of subjecting them to what Laing (1967) so aptly calls "the *degradation* ceremonial of psychiatric examination, diagnosis, and prognostication," by providing places (in the form of retreat communities) where they can enjoy a respite from daily life and refurbish themselves. Given such retreats, one can predict that many of the "symptoms" of "mental illness" will disappear altogether. That is, when people understand that they do not have to appear or render themselves incapacitated, that they can "retreat" whenevery they feel they have to, then they will lose the motivations for symptom expression. Thus, the mere existence and accessibility of these retreats will go a long way toward obliterating the usual accompaniments of "mental illness"—so it is, we think, that many of the "mentally ill" may be "cured."

As we indicated earlier, we cannot hope to eliminate the strains of modern society; life is hard and people will suffer from its stresses. What our solution makes possible, however, is that we will not have to compound a person's difficulties by making him a malingerer; there would be no need to become one if these escape hatches were provided.

Once this society recognizes its obligation to provide temporary relief for some and permanent refuge for others, then retreats such as those we propose become not an extra burden on society but an indispensable requisite in order for any society to flourish. Indeed, it is what any member of society has a right to expect.

COOPERATIVE RETREATS:
OUR PROPOSED SOLUTION

We have suggested that retreat communities be made available to the public, but we have not yet clearly specified what they would be like, what facilities and staff would be there, and so on. We are aware that in some countries retreats similar to those we have envisioned are beginning to be established, but rather than attempting to describe the many variations, we shall present a "model" of the cooperative retreat that incorporates what we consider the ideal qualities.

With the aid of public and private funds, retreats would be set up to service particular communities or regions, much in the way that mental hospitals presently do. Any member of a community, when he desires, may go to the cooperative retreat and stay as long as he wants, at no cost to him, providing there is space enough. The retreat would be structured so that residents may pursue their own preferred life styles—it would be the Everyman's resort. Persons who wish to remain permanent residents may participate, in some personally suitable fashion, in the running of the establishment, thereby reducing the need for employment of outside help. Persons, however, who do not want to work will not be required to do so. Those who want only temporary relief, on the other hand, may make use of the facilities of the retreat in much the same way that more affluent persons use resorts.

Because this is not a treatment community and, accordingly, because it nullifies psychiatrists' *raison d'être*, the professional personnel would be limited to a general medical physician and a hotel management expert. In addition, other persons such as artisans, teachers, and artists may be employed in order to provide as wide a range as possible of activities that may be desired by those attending.

These retreats, small communities situated in the countryside, would have facilities for both the enhancement and entertainment of the residents such as libraries, tennis courts, music recitals, movies, and so on. In short, we would hope to provide a full scope of activities generally pursued in leisure time only. Any organized group activity, such as a seminar or a ball game, would be initiated, planned, and executed by the residents rather than by any staff functionary. For some who enter the retreat, then, new areas of enjoyment and fulfillment may be opened to them, and things they had never before had the opportunity to explore will be accessible.

Thus, as we see it, the cooperative retreat will be an experiment in living for those who come there. It will be for many people a chance to be a member, if only for a short while, of a small, stable, and democratic community where one is free to choose for himself what he would like to do, free to explore the limits of his potentials in order to live a more personally satisfying life.

But if these retreats will be so idyllic, what will prevent mass defections from society? Why would anyone want to live on the outside if such retreats become available? Questions such as these, which have been repeatedly raised, make clear our assertion that life in society today is very difficult and, for many, unfulfilling and misery-laden. But we are hopeful that such retreats would ameliorate the adverse effects of society. We feel that merely knowing that one can "get away from it all" somehow makes life much more bearable. Moreover, visits to retreats would act, we think, as a shot of "social adrenalin," reviving those who come and enabling them, upon return to their communities, to be more fruitful and productive citizens.

For those who simply cannot return to society, either because they lack the skills or because society casts them out, (for example, old or lame people), the retreat will represent for them a home, a place where they can maintain (or develop) self-respect and dignity by functioning in their own way as useful and needed members of the cooperative retreat.

A model retreat such as this will offer freedom to the participants in, who are also the victims of, the double hypocrisy existing today. Patients will no longer have to degrade themselves by acting "crazily"; professional persons will no longer have to intellectuality divorce themselves from reality in order to justify their role; and society will no longer have to misdirect its energies and resources in defense of a myth. "The myth of mental illness" will no longer enable a complacent society to misconceive utterly the nature of one of its most crucial problems. The elimination of this mythology will remove the camouflage used to obscure for too long the real problems facing society. Only then will society be able to embark upon appropriate reforms that will enhance and enrich the lives of its citizens.

Questionnaires

HOSPITAL OPINION INVENTORY

1. The doctors in the hospital never make mistakes about anything.
2. Without exception, every single nurse and aide in the hospital is as good to patients as a mother or father would be to their child.
3. Every meal I have had in the hospital has been as good if not better than meals one gets in a good restaurant.
4. I have never been asked to do things I didn't like while being a patient here.
5. There is nothing about the hospital that needs improvement of any kind.
6. Medication sometimes makes a patient ill.
7. Some of the hospital rules are really not necessary.
8. I have had the thought at times that the hospital doesn't help some patients very much.
9. There are times I have done things in the hospital that the aides or nurses don't know about.
10. I sometimes cover up my true feelings when I talk to a doctor or nurse.
11. I like everyone I ever met at this hospital.
12. I am proud of being a patient in this hospital.
13. The hospital wards are almost as nice as living in a good hotel.
14. There is nothing that the hospital won't do to make a patient happy and comfortable.
15. All patients who get sent to the closed ward deserve to since the hospital is always fair in its decisions.

16. I agree with everything the hospital wants me to do.
17. There are times when I wish the hospital treated me better.
18. Sometimes the hospital staff does not want to be bothered by patients.
19. There are times when I feel that some of the hospital staff do not quite understand me.
20. Sometimes the hospital treats patients as if they were not adults.
21. This hospital is not fit for people who need help.
22. I have never had a single decent meal in the hospital.
23. Sometimes the hospital does some good for patients.
24. There are times when a patient needs to be put on a closed ward.
25. There are times when the hospital staff is right even though a patient may think they are wrong.
26. There is not a single good thing about being a patient in this hospital.
27. I can't find one meaningful and interesting thing to do in this hospital.
28. The hospital always takes advantage of patients.
29. I have to admit that at times I feel comfortable being in the hospital.
30. In some ways I receive more attention in the hospital than I got on the outside.

MENTAL ILLNESS AND SELF-INSIGHT INVENTORY

1. I am easily awakened by noise.
2. Once in a while I put off until tomorrow what I ought to do today.
3. I have met problems so full of possibilities that I have been unable to make up my mind about them.
4. Sometimes when I am not feeling well I am cross.
5. I enjoy a race or a game better when I bet on it.
6. Often I can't understand why I have been so cross or grouchy.
7. I am against giving money to beggars.

8. It is hard for me to ask help from my friends when I cannot return the favor.
9. I gossip a little at times.
10. I have not been very independent or free from family rule.
11. I like to be with a crowd who plays jokes on one another.
12. Once a week or more often I become very excited.
13. I drink an unusually large amount of water every day.
14. I wish I were not bothered by thoughts about sex.
15. There was a time in my life when I liked to play with dolls.
16. I have sometimes stayed away from another person.
17. At periods my mind seems to work more slowly than usual.
18. I have often met people who were supposed to be experts who were no better than I.
19. At times I have worn myself out by undertaking too much.
20. I am often so annoyed when someone tries to get ahead of me in a line of people that I speak to him about it.
21. I have had some unusual religious experiences.
22. I have at times had to be rough with people who were rude or annoying.
23. I am embarrassed by dirty stories.
24. People generally demand more respect for their own rights than they are willing to allow for others.
25. I often memorize numbers that are not important (such as automobile licenses, etc.).
26. I must admit that I have at times been worried beyond reason over something that did not matter.
27. I do not try to cover up my poor opinion or pity of a person so that he won't know how I feel.
28. Some of my family have quick tempers.
29. It makes me angry to have people hurry me.
30. My skin seems to be unusually sensitive to touch.

HOSPITAL INFORMATION TEST I

1. (a) What is the name of your psychiatrist?
   (b) What floor is his or her office on?

2.   What is the name of a nurse in your building?

3. (a) What is the name of the doctor in charge of your building?
   (b) What floor is his office on?

4. (a) What is the name of the nursing supervisor in your building?
   (b) What floor is her office on?

5. (a) What is the name of the psychologist in your building?
   (b) What floor is his office on?

6. (a) What is the name of the social worker in your building?
   (b) What floor is his or her office on?

7. (a) What is the name of the superintendent of this hospital?
   (b) What building is his office in?

8.   How many floors are in your building?

9.   What is the name of the chapel building?

10.   What is the name of the occupational therapy building (OT)?

11.   What is the name of the administrative office building?

12.   What is the name of the movie theatre building?

13.   What building is the canteen in?

14.   What are the visiting days?

15.   What are the visiting hours?

16.   In which way were you admitted to the hospital? (Check one)
          a. Voluntary admission ——
          b. 30-day or emergency commitment ——
          c. Court order ——
          d. Transfer from another institution ——

17.   Make a guess as to how many patients are living in your building.

18.   Make a guess as to many patients are in the entire hospital.

19.   What time does the day shift of aides and nurses leave?

HOSPITAL INFORMATION TEST II

1. (a) What is the name of your psychiatrist?
   (b) What floor is his or her office on?

2.   What is the name of a psychiatrist in
        a. Building "A"
        b. Building "B"
        c. Building "C"

3. (a) What is the name of a nurse in your building?
   (b) What floor is her office on?

4.   What is the name of a nurse in:
        a. Building "A"
        b. Building "B"
        c. Building "C"

5. (a) What is the name of the doctor in charge of your building?
   (b) What floor is his office on?

6.   What is the name of the doctor in charge of
        a. Building "A"
        b. Building "B"
        c. Building "C"

7. (a) What is the name of the nursing supervisor in your building?
   (b) What floor is her office on?

8.   What is the name of the nursing supervisor in
        a. Building "A"
        b. Building "B"
        c. Building "C"

9. (a) What is the name of the psychologist in your building?
   (b) What floor is his office on?

10.   What is the name of a psychologist in
        a. Building "A"
        b. Building "B"
        c. Building "C"

11. (a) What is the name of the social worker in your building?
   (b) What floor is his or her office on?

12.   What is the name of a social worker in
        a. Building "A"
        b. Building "B"
        c. Building "C"

13. (a) What is the name of the Superintendent of this hospital?
   (b) What building is his office in?

14.   How many floors are in your building?

15.   What is the name of the chapel building?

16.   What is the name of the occupational therapy building (OT)?

17.   What is the name of the administrative office building?
18.   What is the name of the movie theatre building?
19.   What building is the canteen in?
20.   What are the visiting days?
21.   What are the visiting hours?
22.   Make a guess as to how many patients are living in your building.
23.   Make a guess as to how many patients are in the entire hospital.
24.   How much vacation time does a state employee get?
25. (a)   How many nursing shifts do they have in the hospital?
    (b)   What are their times?
26.   What is your diagnosis?
27.   What medication do you receive? (Name and amount)
28.   Where can you get good used clothing in the hospital?
29. (a)   What is the name of the hospital magazine?
    (b)   How often is it published?
30.   What are the library hours?
31.   How many libraries are there in the hospital?
32.   Where are they located?
33.   Where are the patient dances held?
34.   What is the name of the medical and surgical building?
35.   Where is the out-patient clinic?
36.   Where is the main dental office?
37.   Who is business manager?
38.   Where is he?
39.   Where is the hospital post office?
40.   Where is the hospital garage?
41.   Who is the head of the OT department?
42.   Who is the head of the nursing department?
43.   Where is the hospital pharmacy?
44.   Where is the police department?
45.   Who is head of social service?
46.   Where is the hospital switchboard?
47. (a)   Who is head of volunteers?
    (b)   Where is she?
48.   Where is the bowling alley?
49.   Where is the gym?
50.   Where is the pool?
51.   Where is the music department?
52.   Where is the school?

53.   Where is the gift shop?
54.   Where is the laboratory?
55.   Where is the swank shop?
56.   What are the names of buildings in which employees live?
57.   Where is the printing shop?
58.   Where is the psychology department?
59.   Where is the shoe repair shop?
60.   Where is the tailor shop?

PATIENT ATTITUDE TEST

The statements that follow are opinions or ideas about mental illness, mental patients, and some general topics. By *mental illness,* we mean the kinds of illness that bring patients to mental hospitals, and by *mental patients* we mean mental hospital patients. There are many differences of opinion about this subject. In other words, many people agree with each of the following statements while many people disagree with each of these statements. We would like to know what *you* think about these statements. Each is followed by six choices:

strongly
agree _____   agree _____   not sure but
                                          probably agree _____

not sure but   strongly
probably disagree _____ disagree _____ disagree _____

Please check in the space provided the choice that comes closest to saying how you feel about each statement. You can be sure that many people will agree with your choice. There are no right or wrong answers: we are interested only in *your opinion.* It is very important that you answer *every* item. [Answer spaces have been omitted and only the statements appear below.]

1. More tax money should be spent in the care and treatment of people with severe mental illness.

2. Anyone who tries hard to better himself deserves the respect of others.

3. If our hospitals had enough well-trained doctors, nurses, and aides, many of the patients would get well enough to live outside the hospital.

4. A patient would be foolish not to try to enjoy himself as long as he is in the hospital.

5. In many ways a hospital is just like any other neighborhood you find on the outside.

6. It is important not to think about the life you lead outside the hospital as long as you are a patient.

7. The administrators of mental hospitals should make a strong effort to hire staff members who are able to get along with people.

8. More than anything else, mental patients need the respect and understanding of the staff members who work with them.

9. The best doctors and drugs cannot cure a mental patient unless the patient does everything he can do to help himself.

10. The best way to fit into hospital life is to try and have a good time.

11. If you really want to, it is not too hard to stay in or leave the the hospital.

12. It's possible to have a good and full life in the hospital while you are a patient.

13. Although patients discharged from mental hospitals may seem all right, they should not be allowed to marry.

14. The best way to handle patients in mental hospitals is to keep them behind locked doors.

15. Regardless of how you look at it, patients with severe mental illness are no longer really human.

16. Once a mental patient, always a mental patient.

17. It's important for a mental patient to have a sense of humor.

18. There is nothing wrong with being a mental patient.

19. There is little that can be done for mental patients in a mental hospital except to see that they are comfortable and well fed.

20. All patients in mental hospitals should be prevented from having children by a painlesss operation.

21. An employer would be foolish to hire a person who has been a patient in a mental hospital, even if he seems fully recovered and is well trained for the job.

22. There are many people on the outside more disturbed than a lot of Old-timers in the hospital.
23. It is good therapy to spend most of your time relaxing and enjoying your stay in the hospital.
24. Medication is more helpful to a patient than individual or group therapy.
25. It is a good thing to treat mental patients with kindness, but it probably will not do much toward helping them get well.
26. It would be hard to develop a close friendship with a person who has been a patient in a mental hospital.
27. People who were once patients in mental hospitals are no more dangerous than the average citizen.
28. A patient should try to make his life as simple as possible while in the hospital.
29. Mental patients should spend time getting to know more about themselves by sitting down alone and thinking.
30. If you want to, it is kind of easy to feel that you are not a patient in a hospital.
31. Most mental patients are willing to work.
32. If the children of mentally ill patients were raised by normal parents, they would probably not become mentally ill.
33. The patients in mental hospitals should have something to say about the way the hospital is run.
34. You have to get to know your doctor if you want to get out of the hospital.
35. The best way to get help for your mental problems is to keep busy and forget you are a patient.
36. Patients in a mental hospital should have as much freedom as they want.
37. It is possible to become mentally ill by believing very strongly that you are likely to suffer eternal punishment and torture after death.
38. There is little use in writing to public officials because they are not really interested in the problems of the average man.
39. Even if a person who has been a patient in a mental hospital seems fully recovered, he should not be given a driver's license.
40. It is important to learn all about the hospital if you want to get things done and enjoy yourself.
41. I don't think there should be mental hospitals but rather only out-patient clinics.

42. Sometimes an aide can be more important in making your stay in the hospital more comfortable than a doctor.
43. Success is more dependent on luck than real ability.
44. Many patients are capable of skilled labor, even though in some ways they are very disturbed.
45. When a person has a problem or a worry, it is best not to think about it, but keep busy with more pleasant things.
46. People with mental illness should never be treated in the same hospital as people with physical illness.
47. There is no excuse for not being in therapy.
48. The only hope for a patient is to get understanding.
49. A woman would be foolish to marry a man who has had a severe mental illness, even though he seems fully recovered.
50. Anyone who is in a hospital for mental illness should not be allowed to vote.
51. Every mental hospital should be surrounded by a high fence and guards.
52. The law should allow a woman to divorce her husband as soon as he has been confined in a mental hospital with a severe mental illness.
53. All most patients need is a period of relaxation to get on their feet again.
54. A patient should not think about leaving but rather about how he can get well again.
55. A person who has been a patient in a mental hospital should not be allowed by law to hold high political office.
56. The main purpose of a mental hospital should be to protect the public from a mentally ill person.
57. Many people in our society are lonely and unrelated to their fellow human beings.
58. Everyone should have someone in his life whose happiness means as much to him as his own.
59. If you want to get well again, it is important to establish a comfortable routine in the hospital.
60. Mental patients should avoid hospital jobs because it makes it easier to want to stay in the hospital.
61. Patients should have more say as to whether they should leave or stay in the hospital.
62. One of the best spots in the hospital is the canteen.
63. As a patient, one shouldn't spend time developing a social life

in the hospital with other patients, especially if the other patients live in other buildings in the hospital.

64. I know of patients who are really well enough to leave, but they enjoy it here and want to stay.

65. If I am discharged, I will try to hide the fact that I was a patient in a mental hospital when I meet new people on the outside.

66. A patient should get to know the staff of the hospital before he starts to get treated for his condition.

67. The best way to learn about the hospital is to ask patients who have been there for some time.

68. A patient should never leave the hospital until he is completely cured.

69. A patient cannot get well unless he is prepared to suffer from his illness.

70. A hospital should not ask a patient to do what he has not done on the outside.

71. Patients will feel better if the hospital does not make any demands.

72. You should try to be on friendly terms with the staff on the ward.

73. Everything a person does in the hospital, including having coffee in the canteen, is therapeutic.

74. Patients should be required to work at a job while they are in the hospital.

75. It would be good for patients if the hospital scheduled all their time in the hospital.

76. Most patients in a state hospital are not mentally ill.

77. Patients would get better if the staff did not bother them.

78. Everybody has a little bit of mental illness in him.

79. Patients should be permitted to go into town whenever they wish to.

80. A patient should try to meet as many other patients as possible rather than limiting himself to patients on his own ward.

81. It is better not to make friends with patients while you are in the hospital.

82. You should always do what the staff wants you to, even if you disagree with them.

83. Watching television is good therapy for a patient.

84. Patients should go to dances because it is a good way to socialize.
85. It is often better not to have visitors from home because they may upset you.
86. Patients always come into the hospital because they are forced to by others.

APPENDIX B

Interviews with
Schizophrenic Patients

NAME: *John Bailey*   AGE: *56*   SEX: *Male*
LENGTH OF PRESENT HOSPITALIZATION: *22 years*

Q. Name as many places in the hospital as you can where a patient can spend time.

A. Well, one, he can spend it on the grounds; two, in any one of the canteens, the library, and, well, mainly on the grounds.

Q. Where on the grounds?

A. Just walking around anywhere, I mean one particular spot is . . . not many of them do it—they used to do it in the old days —you know, that park right in back of the police department. Spend a lot of time there during the summer. It's getting cooler weather now and they mainly, I mean I do, and I know most of the others do, spend most of their time in the building. Then there's Harold Hall and the library and the different facilities they have there. Anything where there's recreation or like that.

Q. Can you name a few specific places?

A. Well, I can't because you can never tell. I mean, I don't go too much to the recreation.

Q. Well, where *can* other patients go?

A. Well, that I would say would be up to the staff where they would hold recreation. Where recreation is, that's what I mean. I tell you truthfully, there's not many other places, unless you sit down around the ball field. That's all. Or you can, if people have trouble with their problems, go over and see the chaplain in the chapel.

Q. Anything else?

A. Well, let's see. I spoke about all the places that I personally would spend my time.

Q. Is there any place in the hospital that a patient can't spend time, that's off-limits?

A. Well, most naturally, where the residents are, such as across the street from the post office and where the staff lives. And most of them know where the off-limits are—and . . . this area down here by the sewerage. And I believe there used to be—I don't know if it still is—area down around in back of . . . you know the area down around the old cow barn? Well, down over the hill there, in that area. Or any area like that.

Q. Are there any other places in the hospital where you spend your time, not necessarily where other patients spend their time?

A. Well, I'm either on the ward, or in the canteen, or walking on the grounds.

Q. What do you do on the ward generally when you're up there?

A. Well, I sit and listen to the radio, or I talk with Fred Smith. I don't watch TV. Once in a while I'll watch TV, but I've had so much TV. I do go to the small canteen, but generally it's the other one. I may have a sandwich, you know, like a hamburg.

Q. Do you go by yourself?

A. Sometimes. Sometimes I invite somebody along, a friend of mine I know hasn't got any money.

Q. On the hospital grounds, where do you spend time?

A. Oh, I tend to spend it not too far from the building, I mean like over across the road here, or I may go down in front here over the bank and lie down.

Q. Do you go to dances?

A. Well, I'm not too hot on dancing, so I don't go to too many of the dances. But I talked to one of the aides, and she's going to teach me to dance, and I may pick up and go to more dances.

Q. Do you go to the movies?

A. No. I'd rather sit and listen to music or the radio or a good radio program.

Q. Is there any place in the hospital that you *have* to go to, that the hospital says you have to be at at a certain time?

A. No, not at present. When I go back to OT for a job or if I get an assignment or, like, group therapy, I have to go there. Then there's rehabilitation.

Q. Let's take your average, typical day and see what your schedule is. What time do you get up?

A. Well, between 6:30 and 6:45, sometimes earlier. But it's generally about 6:30. I wash up and get ready for breakfast. It's generally around 7. After, I participate in ward work, cleaning up the ward until about 8. Then sometimes I go out on details. Not often. Well, like this morning, they have a habit of it, but they know the help is available there and good help. They called the ward, and, like, this morning, I cleaned the multipurpose room. After the dance, or any special assignment.

Q. Well, when there isn't any special assignment, what do you do?

A. Well, I sit and talk or listen to radio or have a coffee.

Q. Where do you typically spend time after breakfast?

A. I spend most of my time on the ward.

Q. Until about what time, on the average?

A. Well, if I haven't got a detail, I generally spend about two-thirds of my mornings, say, from 9 to 10, then I go out for a walk for half to three-quarters of an hour, and then I'll go back to the ward about 11 for medication. Then I wait for dinner on the ward about 11:30.

Q. What do you do typically after dinner?

A. Well, as I say, if I haven't got a detail, I just do what I did in the morning. Oh, I might sit and talk for an hour and then come back and talk and sit and listen to the radio.

Q. When do you go to the canteen? How often do you go there?

A. Well, when I go to the canteen is generally after a detail or on Saturday.

Q. So, when you don't have a detail you spend your time on the ward.

A. That's right.

Q. So, after dinner you spend most of your time on the ward.

A. Typically.

Q. What do you do after suppertime, generally?

A. Well, I mean about the same thing: socialize, listen to the radio. . . . I generally take a walk outside for the last few minutes that we have privileges.

Q. Do you get special assignments very often?

A. Well, no, seeing as I haven't got a regular detail.

Q. I see. OK. So, do you do much visiting in the hospital?

A. Oh, such as?

Q. I mean visit other patients in other buildings.

A. Well, I visit the post office and the old gang. I go over and talk.

Q. And how often do you do that?

A. Oh, maybe once, maybe twice a week.

Q. Do you have friends in other buildings besides the post office?

A. Well, I have some that I know but I haven't seen. . . . See, I've been in different buildings, and I know a lot of the different patients, but I don't go and visit the old—I haven't been going to visit my old friends. If I see them, I sit and talk with them. I like to sit and talk and listen to the radio.

Q. And you spend most of the time by yourself?

A. Well, socially going along, unless Fred Smith is there to talk with, I'd rather sit and listen to the radio. They have a side room and they have a radio in there.

Q. Are there generally many patients in there listening?

A. No, they're generally watching television.

Q. What's a mental hospital supposed to do?

A. Well, it's first supposed to straighten you out so that you can receive some kind of therapy. And then the therapy is to get you to develop so that you can get back outside, and you might be well, but if you realize the changing difference in your social . . . I don't mean drop it altogether, but changing your social living outside would help it a lot. It tends, well, I don't say that it tends, it. . . . The idea is to straighten you out so that you can adapt to social living outside.

Q. How is the patient supposed to get better in the hospital?

A. Well, in one way, it's to cooperate, to go along with whatever is suggested in the line of therapy.

Q. What is a patient supposed to do while he's in the hospital?

A. Well, as I say, go along with therapy, accept the details that they give you, and cooperate in any line. I mean, you might not think that what is suggested you do is going to help you, but in the long run it's probably, I mean, it's not suggested for foolish reasons.

Q. What are psychiatrists for?

A. Psychiatrists are to direct clearing up of your mentality.

Q. How are they supposed to help you?

A. Well, they . . . well, there's your department, psychology. Now he can direct you for therapy. And he can OT for re-establishment of your working abilities and. . . .

Q. What are psychologists for?

A. Well, the full value . . . I think that they work at what is the psychiatric problem that the psychiatrist doesn't have full time to take care of.

Q. What are nurses for?

A. Well, nurses handle medical care and they, with the psychiatric aides, they're trained to know approximately what is supposed to be done, and they can tell what is supposed to be, and they can tell what is advanced, if the patient is advanced in the treatment, whether he might need some other treatment.

Q. What are aides for?

A. Well, aides are to assist the nurse, both in the psychiatric judgment and for restraint, if necessary.

Q. What do you think would happen if there weren't mental hospitals in this country?

A. To tell you truthfully, I don't know what we'd do.

Q. What do you think might happen?

A. Well, we'd be wandering around, and we'd have a lot more Boweries.

NAME: *James Rogers*   AGE: *60*   SEX: *Male*
LENGTH OF PRESENT HOSPITALIZATION: *25 years*

Q. Name as many places in the hospital as you can where a patient can spend time.

A. Well, I would say any. . . . You mean to just sit around?

Q. Yes, where can they go and just sit around?

A. Well, they have their own life. In this building here you can sit around in the lobby, and they got a little place over here, the canteen, and it's got coffee, Coca-Cola. There's no bowling alley in this building. There's one in the other though—Red Hall—it's only two lanes though; there's always waiting. If you want to go to bowl they got a match game going on, you know. You have to get it about two weeks ahead of time when you want a game. They got a swimming pool here, and they got a gymnasium. You got a pool room up there. Well, here you can walk through with permission. You can sit down, watch them play pool or ping pong, and then you can go walk around the buildings. Well, you get permission. Oh yeah, you can go right out of here and walk all around the grounds, you know, as long as you don't get into trouble.

Q. Where else can you go?

A. Well, all around the grounds—you can play softball in the summer, you can go out picking berries, too. They have quite a few strawberries around here. Oh, they picked quite a few last summer. And there's a picnic camp. Course, you can group together and get permission to go to a picnic with the attendants, and they go in the bus or in their cars, and they drive them there. . . . You have to have somebody about 25 anyway, or 30. . . . Oh, they do all right with what they can do with them.

Q. What else can you do?

A. Then they have those dance nights—you get permission from these fellows, from the attendant, and he'll make you up a bit of this orangeade and you know, give it to them to drink, and passing out a few cigarettes. They're pretty good like that.

Q. What else? Are there any other places?

A. Well, you got the library and it's very good. You go up there, they got every newspaper there—the New York papers—and they got magazines, well, you know, what you buy in the stands. They got *Life, Look,* and these other kind, *Esquire,* and a couple of the latest ones out, they got; and people donate magazines . . . and books, they bring them over here.

Q. What other places besides the library?

A. Well, they got an OT building.

Q. What can you do there?

A. Well, that's manual training, like in high school. They have woodcrafts. You ought to take a look at that sometime. Well, between you and me, if you happen to walk around here, you go in there. It's Berrows Hall, it's where the sick hospital is here. But downstairs they got jigsaws. They cut out wood. You can draw out a picture on wood. Did you ever see them do that? And they cut it right out with a saw. That's *occupational therapy.*

Q. Where else can a patient spend time?

A. Well, if they drive you out somewhere, and they get permission and they give you their permission, they drive you out.

Q. What about in the hospital?

A. Well, they got the theater here, they got Adler Hall, they have big dances there, they have a small orchestra with a drum, piano—every Tuesday. And they have the moving pictures upstairs, and downstairs in the cellar is the auditorium, a small auditorium, a small stage.

Q. When do they have the movies?

A. Every Friday night and Friday afternoon—well, with the last show in the Castle Theater up here, they sent a film over here.

Q. Mr. Rogers, can you tell me of any other places?

A. Well, the grounds around here used to be a silver mine once, way over there. Well, they're talking about making a pond out of it. They're digging it all out—what do you call that?—an outside pond. They have an inside swimming pool there. They have it graded out, and they're starting to grow flowers, vegetables around. See, if they want to go out and plant vegetables with the fellow, they'll go out with them. They can go out there two or three hours in the morning; go back about 10. They can have their own farm. And then they can go out there themselves, pick them all up and take them all in if they'll let them use the truck. They can take them in, and I think they'll let them have half of what they get for them.

Well, between me and you, it's only right, 2 cents or 3 cents
on a pound of beets or something like that. That's wonderful
ground over there. I was over there. They got tomatoes that
are that big and round. My father said when they get too
big they don't taste too good, but these are good. We chopped
them up—we had a picnic—and fried them in pans with onions
and they was good. I like fried onions, you know, with po-
tatoes once in awhile.

Q. Is there any other place?

A. Oh, these grounds are pretty big here.

Q. What can patients do on the grounds?

A. They got a tennis court. They go up with permission from a
nurse or attendant.

Q. Is there any place in the hospital where a patient can't spend
time, that is off-limits?

A. What do you mean, just sit around?

Q. Where he can't go. What's off-limits to a patient in a hospital?

A. Oh, I don't know. Well, your off-limits could be permissible
though. Now, if you go in and out of a kitchen here, the guy
will give them a coffee or tea or a hamburger, you know.
That's being kind, and he can do it, though. He can give it
to them. That's his permission, and he's the boss, the chef.
But you can go in and out of that place, and it ain't unpre-
ventable. They don't say don't do it.

Q. So there's no place that you know of that is officially off-limits,
where you can't go?

A. Well, the sick ward. If you want to go in that place to visit,
you got to get permission.

Q. Where do you spend your time in the hospital?

A. Oh well, I'm in and out of the ward here. I work in the laundry til half past 3 in the afternoon. Well, they say you don't
have to work; they'll say if you want to you can, and then
they let you walk around. They kind of privilege you a bit,
and, you know, they're as good to you as they can. . . . Oh,

I go take a walk for myself. Me and another fellow, we go up
to the ball park here, and we sit in the bleachers. Well, now
it's getting a little chilly to play ball, softball; we watch them
play softball. Oh, I'm acquainted a little bit with three out of
the 15 nurses and doctors. The doctors, you know, are in and
out of the buildings. One shook hands with me one time.
"You Rogers?" I says, "Yeah."

Q. What buildings do you go to spend time in?

A. Oh, I got a spot. We play cards, we play pool on the ward. . . .

Q. Where else do you go?

A. The library.

Q. Anywhere else?

A. Oh, I like to sit out here where the canteen is—there's a small
canteen out here . . . and I walk around.

Q. What do you do in the canteen?

A. Oh, sit around drinking coffee.

Q. Alone, or with other people?

A. Other people, of course. You drink one, and one will see you
and he'll buy you one, you buy him one, and then another
buys the three of you one.

Q. Do you have friends that you can talk to?

A. Yeah, they're pretty friendly.

Q. Where can you spend time on the grounds?

A. Where can you? You just walk.

Q. Is there any place in the hospital that you have to be at, that
the hospital says you *have* to spend time at?

A. No.

Q. Let's take your average, typical day. What time do you get up
in the morning?

A. Quarter to 6. I eat sometimes at 7, quarter after 7. After,
go right over to the laundry until quarter after 11. Then I ge

over here, wash up, and eat. Oh, we go back to the laundry again til about 3:30. Then I come over here, play ping pong, or whatever I do.

Q. Where's that, at the multipurpose room?

A. No, the day room. That's only for dancing and meetings, and they have church over there. Well, it's six o'clock before you know it.

Q. So what do you do after that?

A. TV. If it ain't any good, why it's Chinese checkers or something like that. An hour goes quick up there . . . an hour and a half. They can play there that bingo.

Q. Where do they play bingo?

A. Any place around here. They have a sociable night, they play that. If you win, you get a package of cigarettes.

Q. Do you go to the dances?

A. Well, you go. . . . I don't dance though. Oh, I watch them. They have cake.

Q. What's the hospital supposed to do for you?

A. To me! I'm not in, so that leaves me out.

Q. What is the hospital supposed to do?

A. Well, they're not supposed to keep every kind of men in here. See, this hospital is only a place to stay—you know the routine. These other fellows can't work, or they get on the job a couple of days and then quit. They sit around places and they go to sleep in different kind of places, you know.

Q. What is a patient supposed to do while he's in the hospital?

A. Oh, I don't know. They don't do them any harm. Well, they don't get so they can get out and go to work.

Q. How is the hospital supposed to help a patient?

A. Well, like you couldn't say that to anybody, how are they *supposed* to help. You couldn't even print that.

Q. Does it help the patient?

A. Couldn't be sure.

Q. You've been here a long time; you should know.

A. No, I ain't in, so that's all.

Q. But is it supposed to help a patient?

A. Well, I'm supposed to be a judge of a doctor then.

Q. You've seen patients around. Does it help them or doesn't it help them?

A. They don't need no attention in here.

Q. You know patients here who are well and could be taken right out?

A. Right out on the sidewalk. Sure. Well, I ain't saying one out of fifteen and all that. Course, there's fellows here now. I don't mean me. You let them out, get them a job, a position somewhere, and, well, you know. If the job goes so-so, they'll say, well, I think tomorrow will be my last day. You know, they leave the job.

Q. What do doctors do in the hospital?

A. I don't know how good they are.

Q. But what are they for?

A. Just go in and out. If you get sick while you're here.

Q. They help you when you're sick?

A. Oh well, yeah, they get you medicine.

Q. What do psychologists do?

A. For sociabilities, I'd say, wouldn't you?

Q. Do you know what nurses are for?

A. Well, nurses are for, well, when you're sick.

Q. They help you when you're sick.

A. Oh yeah. Prescribe medicine.

Q. What do aides do?

A. Oh, the same thing. They help them out. They're friends, sociables.

Q. Are they the same as nurses?

A. I wouldn't say that.

Q. How are they different?

A. They're good people. They're kind, they're friendly-like. They're OK.

NAME: *Patricia Johnson*   AGE: *34*   SEX: *Female*
LENGTH OF PRESENT HOSPITALIZATION: *6 months*

Q. Name as many places as you can where patients can spend time in the hospital.

A. Do you mean in this building, as a hospital of itself?

Q. No, I mean the whole hospital, including other buildings.

A. The chapel, the canteen.

Q. How about other places, for example in this building?

A. The small canteen, the gym, the music department, the recreation room on the second floor. I can't think of any more.

Q. All right. Now, in these places you mentioned, what do most patients do?

A. Well, in my opinion, they sit around and talk.

Q. I see. In the chapel?

A. Talk. One can get tired of talking.

Q. Well, do they do something else besides talking or is that all they do?

A. Sometimes they listen to music.

Q. What else?

A. The recreation room—they've got pool tables, ping pong, TV; they watch TV, too.

Q. In the recreation room?

A. Yes.

Q. And how about the small canteen? What do most patients do there?

A. Talk some more! Always talking.

Q. Name as many places as you can where a patient cannot spend time in the hospital.

A. All I can think of is in the nursing office on each floor.

Q. Why can't you spend time in the nursing office?

A. That's where they have all the records.

Q. I see. Is that all you can think of?

A. And you can't go into the kitchen.

Q. I see. Why can't you?

A. You'd probably confuse everybody. I mean you'd have 50 people in there talking or doing nothing or jumping around and things like that. And you just can't walk into any doctor's office.

Q. Name the places in the hospital where you spend your time. What do you do?

A. That's easier. Sometimes I go to chapel and talk to Reverend Rogers—once a week usually. I go to the music department almost every day because there I can sit and talk if I want to; I can play an instrument, listen to music; and just about anything I want to do I can do there, and no one throws me out. I used to go to OT, but I don't like the people up there, and it's too busy and too confusing to me. Very unrelaxing. So I don't go there. And then I go to the library sometimes. Want to know why I go there? I look up all kinds of words.

Q. To look up words?

A. Yes. Things I hear around.

Q. In the dictionaries?

A. Yes, in the encyclopedias, too. I find, well, people are always talking about being depressed, mentally ill, emotionally disturbed, and all that, so I look up those things. But it doesn't mean much to me; it doesn't sink in.

Q. Do you mean the library in this building?

A. Yes. So I don't get the latest information; I just get what's in the encyclopedia. They were published in 1957 or something. What else. . . . Sometimes I go to the small canteen. Sometimes I go to the recreation room. What do I do there? Oh, I play pool, sometimes I watch TV. Usually on Sundays they get good programs on. And let's see. . . .

Q. Is that the recreation room in this building?

A. Yes. Second floor, 208. I spend a lot of time talking to Dr. Smith in her office. And sometimes I go over to the OT building where I talk to Sarah Roberts. She's an OT trainee.

Q. When you go to these various places where there are other people sitting, talking, or playing pool in the recreation room or so forth, do you meet your friends there or people you know?

A. Usually. I don't always. Sometimes I talk to people I don't even know; I don't even know their names.

Q. When you go to the small canteen, do you generally go by yourself?

A. By myself.

Q. Do you find people there usually?

A. Yes.

Q. Do you have any special friends?

A. I did, until last week. But I don't have any friends now. Oh, after 4:30 I go down to the lobby and sit and find lots of people who are willing to talk because there's nothing else to do. I usually go out by myself, and then I usually find someone to talk with, but I like to go by myself, walk off in the woods or something. I sit there and write poetry; so I try to get people to leave me alone. But I have to be nice and talk to them.

Q. Where are the places that you must spend time?

A. Well, the ward, my room, from 11 to 6. The ward—I stay there til 8:30, but I can do whatever I want. Well, no, now they've gotten this thing that I have to go to music—I have guitar lessons. That's four times a week, four hours. Then I want to start playing the recorder, and that'll be two hours. And I'm supposed to go to OT, but I don't go. I must do these things, but I don't. And that's it. I don't have to do anything else.

Q. I want to go through your average or typical day to find out what you do usually. So, starting from the morning, what time do you get up?

A. I usually get up about 6:30 and go back to bed until 7. Then I get up again and go to breakfast. I come back, oh, about 7:30. I usually end up talking there. But I have to stay on the ward. I usually leave at 9 because I have to check everybody's work and make sure he did it.

Q. I see. You're the ward chairman.

A. Yes. And then I go to the music department. I don't know—every day is different though. One day I'll go up there and spend the whole day; another day I'll just go there for an hour. Just what I feel like doing.

Q. Well, in the morning, on the average, how much time do you spend in music?

A. Couple of hours. Well, lately I have been going to this little room we have—with my typewriter, and writing things, listening to music, all by myself.

Q. Until dinner time?

A. Yes.

Q. And what do you do after dinner?

A. Usually try and find someone to talk with me, Dr. Smith, Reverend Rogers, anybody. Then after that I feel better, and I go back to the music department, play the guitar a little bit, and talk.

Q. You go back to music about what time?

A. About 2:30. And I stay there until she throws me out at 4:30 or 5. Then I go to supper. And then, after supper, I go and try to find someone who'll play chess with me.

Q. That's 5:30 supper's over?

A. Yes, or quarter to six sometimes. Then I either try to find somebody that'll play chess or write letters.

Q. You do this on the ward?

A. Oh, sometimes I go outside and sit down and write. And let's see, what do I . . . ?

Q. On the average, how much time during the evening do you spend outside the ward?

A. Oh, two and a half hours, three hours, till it's time to come back.

Q. Is that right after supper that you take off?

A. Well, it depends on if I'm going to write or type a letter or something like that. Then I stay on the ward, but otherwise I go out. But at 9 I have to come back, and then I usually try to read the paper or some magazines, and then I start writing again. I write until the night nurse comes on, and then she sends me to bed, and if she's late then I stay up late.

Q. What time do you usually turn in?

A. 11, 11:30.

Q. Do you go visiting in the hospital?

A. I used to.

Q. Do you have friends in other buildings?

A. No, they're all gone now. Oh, once in a while I see somebody in Rogers Hall.

Q. Not very often?

A. No, my best friends have left.

Q. What is the hospital supposed to do, in your opinion?

A. Ha, ha, ha! That's a very good question. I've been asking myself that for five months.

Q. And what did you come up with?

A. Several things. It depends on what's wrong with you. If all
you need to do is get away from somebody that's bothering
you, this is a very fine place to go. And then this place is
maybe just a custodial place—you can't take care of yourself,
so you let other people get you up, make sure you get dressed,
go to meals. And then it's a place you can go when you want
to get away from all stress, you want to hide from the world,
and, in being this way, you're still acceptable to some people
—like people here. Again, it doesn't make any difference what
you do down here; it's expected that you should act crazy because you are. It's a haven. But I guess for some people it's a
place to get some sort of help. Supposed to get some people
to understand you and help you to understand yourself, how
to cope with life and all that.

Q. Well, how does the hospital do this, getting you to understand
yourself, getting you to cope with life?

A. Well, there are various therapies, such as group therapy, individual therapy, and people like Miss Burns who try to help
you understand yourself while you're at the same time learning something new and being occupied in a way and. . . .

Q. What would you do if there wasn't a hospital?

A. Ha, ha, ha! I'd kill myself. I couldn't. I don't know. Well, there
are reasons for that. You see, my parents wouldn't take me
home and let me do nothing, being unuseful. I'd have to live
on my own, and so I just don't give a damn about anything.
And if I was on my own, I'd have a very difficult, almost impossible, time providing for myself, and I would waste away.
Instead of doing that, I would kill myself. Here, if I don't feel
like doing anything, people will do it for me!

Q. Well, what are you supposed to do in the hospital?

A. Nothing!

Q. Anything that you're supposed to do?

A. If you want to, you can do whatever's available.

Q. How are you supposed to get better in the hospital?

A. Very good question! I could tell you what you shouldn't do.

Q. OK. What should you not do?

A. Take people's advice. You should avoid doing that.

Q. Well, what should you do? Can you think of anything?

A. Talk.

Q. You should talk.

A. Yes. Keep talking. Because when I first was sick, I didn't talk. All I did was sit around and do nothing. I didn't even talk, I didn't say anything. I figured that's all I can do, that's what I should do.

Q. What are doctors for? How are they supposed to help you?

A. Oh, God! They're little men; run around making you answer questions. That's all. They're no good.

Q. The nurses? How are they supposed to help you?

A. They keep order around here, give medication, make sure you get medication, get it right and on time. They help you to take interest in something outside yourself, and also they're listeners and try to understand you.

Q. What are aides for?

A. The same thing nurses are for. Only they're a little bit more authoritative.

Bibliography

ARIETI, S., Some aspects of the psychopathology of schizophrenia. *American Journal of Psychotherapy*, 8:396, 1954.

———, *American Handbook of Psychiatry*. New York: Basic Books, Inc., 1959.

ARTISS, K., *The Symptom as Communication in Schizophrenia*. New York: Grune & Stratton, Inc., 1959.

ASCH, S., *Social Psychology*. Englewood Cliffs, N.J.: Prentice-Hall, Inc., 1952.

BECKER, E., *The Revolution in Psychiatry*. London: Collier-Macmillan, Ltd., 1964.

BELLAK, L., *Schizophrenia: A Review of the Syndrome*. New York: Logos Press, 1958.

BIERER, J., The therapeutic community hostel. *International Journal of Social Psychiatry*, Winter, 1960–1961.

BRAGINSKY, B., J. HOLZBERG, D. RIDLEY, AND D. BRAGINSKY, Patient styles of adaptation to a mental hospital. *Journal of Personality*, 36:283–298, 1968.

BRAGINSKY, B., AND D. BRAGINSKY, Schizophrenic patients in the psychiatric interview: An experimental study of their effectiveness at manipulation. *Journal of Consulting Psychology*, 21:543–547, 1967.

———, M. GROSSE, AND K. RING, Controlling outcomes through impression-management: An experimental study of the manipulative tactics of mental patients. *Journal of Consulting Psychology*, 30:295–300, 1966.

———, J. HOLZBERG, L. FINISON, AND K. RING, Correlates of the mental patient's acquisition of hospital information. *Journal of Personality*, 35:323–342, 1967.

BROCKOVEN, J., AND A. SARBOURNE, *Moral Treatment in American Psychiatry.* New York: Springer-Verlag, 1963.

CONANT, J., *On Understanding Science.* New Haven, Conn.: Yale University Press, 1947.

DAHLSTROM, W., AND G. WELSH, *An MMPI Handbook.* Minneapolis: University of Minnesota Press, 1960.

DAVIS, K., Mental hygiene and the class structure. *Psychiatry, 1*:55–65, 1938.

DEUTSCH, A., *The Mentally Ill in America,* 2d ed. New York: Columbia University Press, 1949.

DOWNING, J., Chronic mental hospital dependency as a character defense. *Psychiatric Quarterly, 32*:489–499, 1958.

EYSENCK, H., *Handbook of Abnormal Psychology.* New York: Basic Books, Inc., 1961.

———, *The Effects of Psychotherapy.* New York: International Science Press, 1966.

FAIRWEATHER, G., *Social Psychology in Treating Mental Illness: An Experimental Approach.* New York: John Wiley & Sons, Inc., 1964.

FOUCAULT, M., *Madness and Civilization: A History of Insanity in the Age of Reason.* New York: Pantheon Books, Inc., 1965.

GOFFMAN, E., *The Presentation of Self in Everyday Life.* New York: Doubleday & Company, Inc., 1959.

———, *Asylums.* New York: Doubleday & Company, Inc., 1961.

GORDON, H., AND L. GROTH, Mental patients wanting to stay in the hospital. *American Medical Association Archives of General Psychiatry, 4*:124–130, 1961.

GRAYSON, H. M., AND L. B. OLINGER, Simulation of "normalcy" by psychiatric patients on the MMPI. *Journal of Consulting Psychology, 21*:73–77, 1957.

HALEY, J., The art of being schizophrenic. *Voices, 1*:133–147, 1965.

HELFAND, I., Role taking in schizophrenia. *Journal of Consulting Psychology, 20*:37–41, 1956.

HOFFER, E., *The Passionate State of Mind.* New York: Harper & Row, Publishers, 1954.

———, *The Ordeal of Change*. New York: Harper & Row, Publishers, 1963.

———, *The Temper of Our Time*. New York: Harper & Row, Publishers, 1967.

JOINT COMMISSION ON MENTAL ILLNESS AND HEALTH. *Action for Mental Health*. New York: Basic Books, Inc., 1961.

JONES, E., *Ingratiation*. New York: Appleton-Century-Crofts, 1964.

JONES, M., *The Therapeutic Community: A New Treatment Method in Psychiatry*. New York: Basic Books, Inc., 1953.

KENISTON, K., *The Uncommitted: Alienated Youth in American Society*. New York: Harcourt, Brace & World, Inc., 1965.

KUHN, T., *The Structure of Scientific Revolutions*. Chicago: University of Chicago Press, 1962.

LAING, R., *The Politics of Experience*. New York: Pantheon Books, Inc., 1967.

LEVINSON, D., AND E. GALLAGHER, *Patienthood in the Mental Hospital*. Boston: Houghton-Mifflin Company, 1964.

LORR, M., Multidimensional scale for rating psychiatric patients. *Veterans Administration Technical Bulletin, 51*:119–127, 1953.

LUDWIG, A., AND F. FARRELLY, The code of chronicity. *Archives of General Psychiatry, 15*:562–568, 1966.

———, The weapons of insanity. *American Journal of Psychotherapy, 4*:737–749, 1967.

MILLER, D., Worlds that fail. *Transaction,* 36–41, December 1967.

MOWRER, O. H., "Sin," the lesser of two evils. *American Psychologist, 15*:301–304, 1960.

MOWRY, R. S., in G. Fairweather, *Social Psychology in Treating Mental Illness: An Experimental Approach*. New York: John Wiley & Sons, Inc., 1964.

PALMER, M., Social rehabilitation for mental patients. In S. Spitzer and N. Denzin (eds.), *The Mental Patient*. New York: McGraw-Hill, Inc., 1968.

PHILLIPS, L., Case history data and prognosis in schizophrenia. *Journal of Nervous and Mental Diseases, 117*:515–525, 1953.

RAKUSIN, J., AND L. FIERMAN, Five assumptions for treating chronic psychotics. *Mental Hospitals, 14*:140–148, 1963.

REDLICH, F., AND D. FREEDMAN, *The Theory and Practice of Psychiatry.* New York: Basic Books, Inc., 1966.

SARBIN, T., Anxiety: The reification of a metaphor. *Archives of General Psychiatry, 10*:630–638, 1964.

———, On the futility of the proposition that some people be labeled "mentally ill." *Journal of Consulting Psychology, 31*:447–453, 1967a.

———, The concept of hallucination. *Journal of Personality, 35*:359–380, 1967b.

———, The scientific status of the mental illness concept. In S. Plog (ed.), *Determinants of Mental Illness—A Handbook.* New York: Holt, Rinehart and Winston, Inc., 1967c.

———, Role theoretical analysis of schizophrenia. In J. H. Mann (ed.), *Reader in General Psychology.* Skokie, Ill.: Rand McNally & Company, 1967d.

———, Notes on the transformation of social identity. In N. S. Greenfield, M. L. Miller, and L. M. Roberts (eds.), *Comprehensive Mental Health: The Challenge of Evaluation.* Madison, Wis.: University of Wisconsin Press, 1967e.

SCHEFF, T. J., *Being Mentally Ill: A Sociological Theory.* Chicago: Aldine, 1966.

SCHOOLER, C., AND D. PARKEL, The overt behavior of chronic schizophrenics and its relationship to their internal state and personal history. *Psychiatry, 29*:67–77, 1966.

STANTON, A., AND M. SCHWARTZ, *The Mental Hospital.* New York: Basic Books, Inc., 1954.

STEARNS, A., AND A. ULLMAN, One thousand unsuccessful careers. *American Journal of Psychiatry, 11*:801–809, 1949.

STRUENING, E., AND J. COHEN, Opinions about mental illness in personnel of two large mental hospitals. *Journal of Abnormal and Social Psychology, 64*:349–360, 1962.

SZASZ, T., Psychiatry, ethics and the criminal law. *Columbia Law Review,* 58:183–198, 1958.

———, *The Myth of Mental Illness.* New York: Paul B. Hoeber, Inc., 1961.

————, *Law, Liberty, and Psychiatry: An Inquiry into the Social Uses of Mental Health Practices.* New York: Crowell-Collier and Macmillan, Inc., 1963.

————, *Psychiatric Justice.* New York: Crowell-Collier and Macmillan, Inc., 1965.

TOWBIN, A., Understanding the mentally deranged. *Journal of Existentialism,* 7:63–83, 1966.

————, The Self-Care Unit: Some Lessons in Institutional Power and Communication. Unpublished Manuscript, 1968.

TRYON, R., Reliability and behavior domain validity: Reformulation and historical critique. *Psychological Bulletin,* 54:229–249, 1957.

VAIL, D., *Mental Health Systems in Scandinavia.* Springfield, Ill.: Charles C Thomas, Publisher, 1968.

WINER, B., *Statistical Principles in Experimental Design.* New York: McGraw-Hill, Inc., 1962.

ZILBOORG, G., AND G. HENRY, *A History of Medical Psychology.* New York: W. W. Norton & Company, Inc., 1941.

Index

Hospital Opinion Inventory, 54, 187
Hospital staff information, 80, 82, 83, 85–88, 90, 92, 94, 95, 97, 104
Hospitalization, 3, 5–8, 49, 58, 81, 98, 141–143, 151, 180, 181
    length of, 6, 36, 64, 81, 87, 88, 91–93, 95, 96, 109
    See also Institutionalization

Impression management, 29, 34, 51–53, 58–60, 63–66, 69, 70, 73, 112, 159, 172
Information acquisition, 80, 81, 83, 85, 87, 88, 91, 94, 95, 100, 110
Ingratiation, 53, 55–59, 65, 159
Institutionalization, 3, 4, 77, 112, 128, 142, 162, 165, 167, 170–172, 179
    See also Hospitalization
Interaction, 80, 93, 94, 112, 116, 117
Interviews, patient, 7, 15, 66, 67, 199

Joint Commission on Mental Illness and Health, 5, 27, 64

Kuhn, Thomas, 28, 35, 38, 44, 174

Labeling, 4, 6, 8, 43
Leisure time, 131, 132, 135, 161, 162, 170, 185

Manipulative tactics, 70, 71, 160
Mental health centers, 7, 9
Mental hospitals, 3, 7, 9, 54, 58, 132, 157, 160, 163, 171, 180, 182
    See also Residential aspects, Resort potentials
Mental illness, 3–5, 8, 9, 27, 58, 69, 163, 170, 171, 174, 177, 178, 182, 184
    dominant conceptions of, 27–30, 77, 112, 128, 174, 178, 179, 182

Mental Illness Test, 60, 188
Mental patients, attitudes of, 88, 95, 104, 105, 110, 151
    modal, 121, 124, 127, 165
    motility of, 99
    motivation of, 4, 6, 7, 29, 52, 55, 59, 72, 73, 80, 113, 159, 160, 172
        See also Hedonistic motivation
    psychiatrist contact with, 114, 116, 119, 120
        See also Goals, patient; Discharge of mental patients
Mental status interviews, 67, 69, 70, 71
Miller, D., 2, 169
Minnesota Multiphasic Personality Inventory (MMPI), 36, 59
Mobile socializers, 100, 104, 105, 110, 111, 117
Mowry, R. S., 37
The Myth of Mental Illness, 41

Newcomers, 59, 63, 172
    See also First-admission patients

Old-timers, 59, 63, 68, 93, 110, 135, 142, 143, 172
Open ward patients, 67, 69–71
Opinions about Mental Illness Scale (OMI), 81, 82, 88, 98

Patient Attitude Test (PAT), 98, 124, 133–135, 142, 193
Phillips Premorbid Adjustment Scale, 82, 96, 133, 134, 141
Power, legitimate, 50, 51, 77
    subversive, 50, 51, 53
    See also Counterpower
Psychiatric model, 2, 9, 10
Psychiatric perspective, 38, 39, 44, 45
Psychological ecology of the hospital, 98